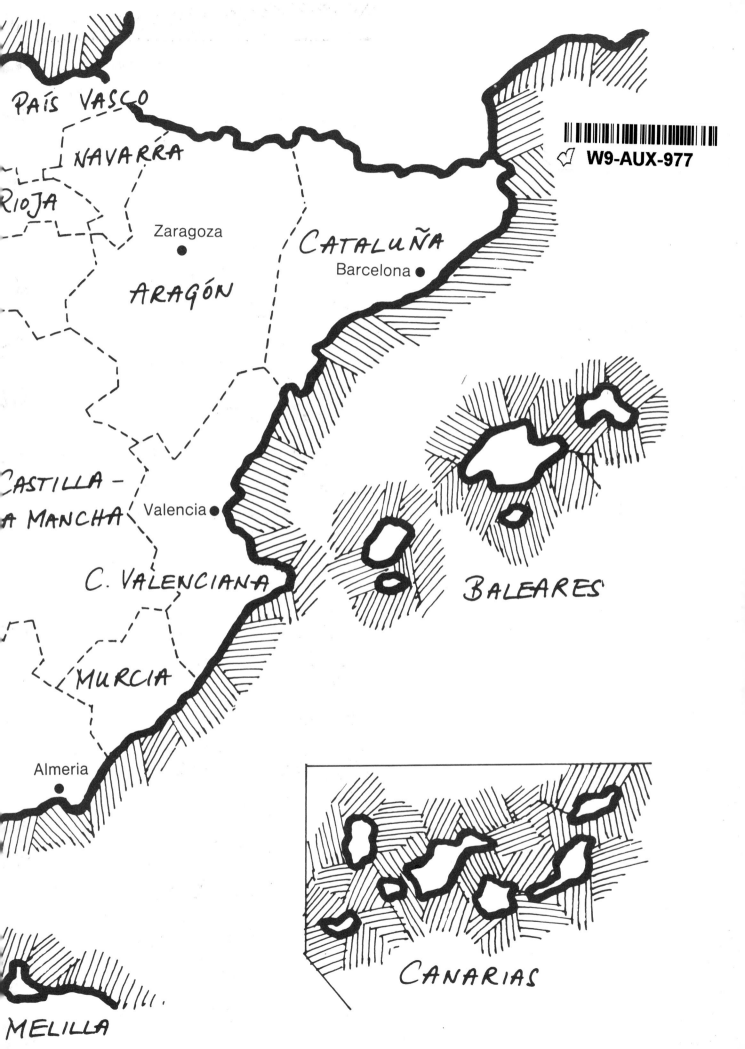

PAÍS VASCO

NAVARRA

RIOJA

Zaragoza

CATALUÑA

Barcelona

ARAGÓN

CASTILLA - A MANCHA

Valencia

C. VALENCIANA

BALEARES

MURCIA

Almeria

CANARIAS

MELILLA

Mosaik

Néstor and Tin Luján

Spain

A gourmet tour
of the regions

Design: Hubertus von Baer, Freising
Recipe editor: Tina Peters
Text editor: Jürgen Trüol
Additional material: Dr. Friedhelm Mühleib (pp. 154-156)
Translation and adaptation: UPS Translations, London

Photos: A.G.E. Foto-Stock: pp. 11, 16, 17, 33 (above and
below right), 34, 35 (both), 45 (left), 59, 70/71, 80, 81, 92,
104, 106, 107, 108, 121, 122, 123, 134, 135, 148/149, 149
(above); Alfa Omega: pp 12, 13, 19, 33 (above left), 44, 45
(right), 58, 60/61, 68, 69, 80, 82, 82/83, 94, 108/109, 120, 122,
136/137, 149 (above); Bedmar: pp. 34, 71, 84; Gruner & Jahr,
Banderob: pp 150/151, Bog v.d. :p 47, Ruhde: p 8/9; IFA-
Bilderteam, Everts: p. 132/133, Lecom: p. 56/57; Studio
Eising: p. 151; Klammet, Ohlstadt: p. 30/31, 42/43, 66/67,
78/79, 118/119; Helga Lade Photo Agency, Bauer: p. 14/15;
Paco Llobet: p. 20/21, 22/23, 24/25, 26/27, 29, 36/37, 38/39,
40/41, 48/49, 50/51, 53, 54/55, 62/63, 64, 72/73, 75, 86/87,
88/89, 96/97, 100/101, 102/103, 110/111, 113, 114/115,
124/125, 126/127, 128/129, 138/139; Mosaik-Verlag,
Brainier: Pp. 95, 117; Press-Agent, Dukes: p. 141; Go: p. 61
(small photo), 46.

© 1991 Mosaik Books, Munich/5 4 3 2 1
English Edition 1993 published by Mosaik Books,
a division of Geocenter International UK. Ltd.
Typesetting: The Printed Word, London
Printing: EGDSA, Barcelona
D L B. 39712-92
Printed in Spain
ISBN 3-576-80017-4

Contents

PREFACE

In contrast to the two other Latin cuisines, Italian and French, Spanish cuisine has gone relatively unrecognised until recently. Spain has long been the most popular tourist destination in Europe, but the dishes served to tourists were limited to such standard fare as Calamares a la romana or Paella.

Traditional meals were only to be found off the beaten track. Even then, only a few places were able to offer authentic dishes.

Today the situation has changed considerably. The mass tourism trend is reversing. More and more culture-lovers come to visit the historical sites and places of interest. Barcelona and Madrid have become focal points of modern European culture and chefs de cuisine have revived the traditional recipes and methods of preparation. The independent traveller who visits Spain today will once again be able to find the sort of dishes that have been cooked there since time immemorial. Of course nowadays the ingredients are of a higher quality and may sometimes be a little more exotic but their traditional character has been retained.

Of the few cookery books about Spanish cooking currently on the non-Spanish market, as far as we know not one has been written by a Spaniard. The authors have mostly been foreigners who have collected recipes from all over the country. So it seems to make sense to leave the writing of this book to a Spanish husband-and-wife team of authors.

Tin and Nestor Luján are natives of Barcelona and are well-known for having written several cookery books in Spain. Tin Luján manages the richly traditional "Agut d'Avignon" restaurant in Barcelona's Barrio Gótico district. Nestor Luján is a bon viveur and gourmet., who has been editing the "Guía del Viajero" restaurant guide for many years. Many of his articles about the art of cookery have been published in the Spanish press and three years ago he produced a comprehensive history of gastronomy. He is also known to the wider Spanish public as a writer and novelist.

As the Lujáns say in their introduction, there is no such thing as typical Spanish cuisine. Spain is so diverse, having been shaped by so many historical and cultural influences, that it has never developed a homogenous cooking style. It is for this reason that the author has divided Spain into 10 different culinary regions. Each region is given a short general introduction, followed by a selection of recipes for the most typical dishes.

Just as every region has its own character, in addition to its local everyday dishes, it also has a particular speciality, such as the mariscos (shellfish) of Galicia or the peppers of Rioja. The recipes in this book are not fancy, nouvelle cuisine adaptations which merely use Spanish ingredients; they are utterly authentic examples of Spanish cooking which the true lover of Mediterranean food will find most rewarding.

THE CULINARY DIVERSITY OF SPAIN

Spain is a land of variety and contrast. The 17 regions of the Iberian Peninsula are subject to extreme temperature fluctuations. For instance, in the mountainous regions of the north, it can be as cold as –25°C in mid-winter and in southern Andalusia the temperature can rise to over 40°C in high summer. The topography and flora and fauna are remarkably varied, ranging from the alpine regions of the Pyrenees, still inhabited by bears in the North, to the huge sugar plantations and salt mines along the coast near Cadiz and the pink flamingos of the nature reserves in the South.

Spain is surrounded by three seas, the Mediterranean, the Atlantic and the Cantabrian Sea. The warm climate and sandy beaches make Spain a favourite travel destination for sun-and-sand-seeking holidaymakers from northern climes. Year after year, millions of northern Europeans flock to the beaches of the mainland, the Balearics and the Canary Isles.

Last, but by no means least, the people are as varied in their traditions, culture and religious beliefs as is the landscape in which they live. They have created their distinct ways of life, depending on whether they live in the south or the north, in the countryside or the big cities like Madrid or Barcelona. No fewer than four languages are spoken - Castilian, (Castellano) the official language - and the three regional languages, Catalan, Basque and Galician.

The cuisine of the country varies as much as the landscape and the people. It is hard to find an all-embracing definition for it. Spain, unlike France, did not develop a national cuisine between the 17th and 19th centuries. The foods eaten were the product of different regional cuisines, whose diversity has been shaped by its diverse history. Lack of resources on the one hand and mass tourism on the other have forced Spanish restaurants to improvise.

It was mistakenly believed that Spain's visitors would prefer the familiar food of their own country to original Spanish cooking. In those days, only "continental cuisine" or at best a poor imitation of

Page 8/9: Seafood and wine by the sea

Right: The Myrtle Courtyard of the Alhambra.

Iberian cooking was a on offer to the tourist. Consequently, traditional Spanish cuisine suffered a great deal.

In the early 1980s, a movement sprang up in reaction to this trend, which championed the culinary traditions of each particular region. Today, each region is able to offer those visitors who want to sample authentic Spanish food a wide choice of local dishes.

If one were to generalise about Spanish cooking methods and summarise them in one sentence, one could say that, "in the South food is fried, in the centre, it is grilled and in the North, it is boiled". It is essentially the type of ingredients used which distinguish the different regional cuisines, however, they also have much in common. Fish is the main ingredient of regional cooking in the areas bordering on the Mediterranean down to Andalusia. Other basics are vegetables, poultry and especially rice, which was probably introduced to Spain by the Arabs. Cookery books of the Iberian Peninsula will often contain one rice dish for every day of the year. Spanish cookery has several other features in common, such as a preference for cooking with olive oil or lard. Butter is rarely used in traditional Spanish cooking. Only today, via the Common Market ,have butter and margarine-type solid fats been incorporated into the cuisine.

The preference for "cocido", a cross between a broth and a stew, is shared by all the Spanish regions., though each region has developed its own version.In the North, the Catalonian version, Escudella i Carne d'Olla combines poultry, beef and pork with different kinds of vegetables and the local Butifarra sausage, which are replaced by the Chorizo, a spicy paprika sausage, in Madrid, or Morcilla, a blood sausage.The Castilian generally prefers his Puchero with lamb, the Galician prepares his Pote Gallego with pork, whilst the Andalusian Cocido Andaluz is a variation of the Castilian stew.

To summarise, without doubt it is the differences rather than the similarities which make Spanish cooking special. The attraction of many dishes lies in the use of ingredients which are often the specialities of a particular region.

The recipes in this book are intended to introduce the reader to the original, traditional dishes of Spanish cooking.We have specifically chosen those recipes whose ingredients should not prove to be too much of a problem to obtain. We wish you every success and "Que aproveche" - bon appetit!

Left: Traditional stove and fireplace in Aragón.

Below: Even today the camel often serves as a beast of burden.

Unless stated otherwise, all recipes are for four people.

GALICIA

This region lies at the tip of north-western Spain and shares a frontier with Portugal. The coastline is very jagged, as the Atlantic bites deep into it, in a string of bays and capes. The landscape is hilly and criss-crossed with rivers. Galicia was once inhabited by Celts, Swabians and Romans. These ancient races have left their mark both on the countryside and on the local people. The Galicians love music and poetry like their Celtic ancestors. The bagpipes are as popular here as they are in Scotland and Ireland.

People who live along Galician coast eat a lot of fish and shellfish including salmon, turbot,, octopus, squid, spider-crabs, lobster, oysters, mussels and clams. Further inland, hearty fare is more popular, on account of the damper, cooler climate. Even today the feudal and monastic origins of dishes are reflected in Galician eating habits. There are dishes such as lacón con grelos *(cooked, smoked shoulder of pork with turnip greens),* empanadas *(pies filled with meat or fish),* capones de Villalba *(chickens marinated in brandy, a Christmas dish) and the various* potajes, *rich stews of vegetables, meat and fish. One of these, which has a special name, the* caldo gallego, *used to be served at the end of a huge winter feast. The hills of Galicia are rich in game, so there are some delicious game dishes such as wild duck a la Ribadeo, smoked loin of wild boar and fricassee of partridge.*

The Galicians are also fond of deserts and pastries. There are filloas, *a kind of pancake made of flour and eggs, which nowadays are filled with custard or cream. In days of old they were very popular at Mardi Gras time, when pigs' blood was added to the mixture. This ritual was supposedly symbolic of the festive spirit before the meatless fast of Lent. Filloas definitely taste better with whipped cream!*

Overleaf p.14/15: Typical Galician landscape near Castro Caldas.

Left: Gathering mussels on La Toja beach.

Right: Statue of St. James the Apostle, the patron saint of Spain, in the Cathedral of Santiago de Compostela.

16

Shellfish - a Galician Speciality

Galician cuisine is completely devoid of Arab influence because the Moors never reached this remote land at the north-western tip of the Iberian peninsula, whose damp climate they considered too harsh. In fact the food of the Spanish coastal regions differ considerably from that of other regions.

Spanish fish is generally of excellent quality, especially the Galician molluscs, crustaceans and cuttlefish. Shellfish figures prominently in Galician cooking along the province's jagged coastline. A careful choice of the ingredients provides the foundations for an outstanding meal. In the fish markets of Vigo and La Coruña, housewives carefully scrutinise the catch, which will eventually be served up and enjoyed at huge dinner tables for the big Sunday family meal.

The oyster has a close association with Galicia. It is a prized delicacy, and oyster-farming has been practised for a very long time. An amazing discovery was made on the two thousandth anniversary of the founding of the city of Lugo; an ancient city wall was unearthed which was found to be in surprisingly excellent condition. These walls had been cemented with mortar made from hundreds of tons of oyster shells. Another interesting historical fact is that as early as the 18th century, pickled oysters were exported to England. The excellence of these oysters was then famous throughout Europe .Today the Galician oyster can compete in quality with the best in the world.

As for scallops, these were once so abundant that they were the staple diet of the poor. This was the reason why an inn frequented by poor men was known as a *mesón de vieiras* (The scallop inn). This is how the scallop shell came to be associated with the pilgrimage to the greatest cathedral in Spain which happens to be in Galicia, St. James (Santiago) of Compostela. Pilgrims would wear scallop shells in their hats to prove that they had made the pilgrimage. That was long ago; in the meantime, the scallop has experienced a considerable rise in prestige. Nowadays a plate of this delicacy ranks amongst the finest and most expensive dishes Galician cuisine has to offer. No less prized is *percebada*, a dish of goose-barnacles boiled and seasoned with a pinch of paprika. This is a simple method of preparation, but the fact is that the quality of Galician shellfish has always been so good and their natural taste so exquisite that neither the fishermen on the boats nor the housewives in the kitchen have felt inclined to invent complicated recipes for them. Thus shellfish are almost always served simply boiled in salted water.

A Galician restaurant called "*El Pescador*" (The Fisherman'), is almost guaranteed to serve excellent food. Around the north coast of Spain, the Atlantic proves to be a treasure-trove, a veritable storehouse for the gourmet of shrimps, crabs, crawfish (langoustine), lobster, scallops, clams, tuna fish and squid. A greater abundance of fish would be hard to find anywhere else in Europe. It goes without saying that the Galicians are masters when it comes to cooking seafood.

Naturally, garlic plays a major role in the preparation. Fish are also flavoured with chives, pepper, rosemary and thyme, whilst saffron and lemon help to bring out the delicate flavour of without smothering it. And to accompany these treats from the sea, how satisfying when one rolls a chilled mouthful of a cold Penedès, the white wine from the vineyards south of Barcelona, over one's tongue.

The greatest culinary delights that Galicia has to offer are swimming in the sea and settled at the tidemark along its intricate coastline. The distinctive character of this region will be served up to you on a plate.

Goose-barnacles are cut loose from the jagged Galician cliffs in extremely dangerous conditions.

ENSALADA DE LUBRIGANTE CON BERROS

Lobster and Watercress Salad

Lobster is the king of Galician crustaceans. Its exquisite flesh tastes even better when combined with a watercress salad.

2 x 600 g/1½ lb lobsters	250 ml/8 fl oz olive oil
125 ml/4 fl oz olive oil	
3 bunches watercress	4 tablespoons (60 ml) fish
2 turnips	stock
8 radishes	
1 clove garlic, peeled	**Wine:** a light sparkling,
Salt	young white wine such as
4 mint leaves	B. Penedès, Albariño or
1 lemon, juice squeezed	Cava

If the lobsters are uncooked, bring plenty of salted water to the boil. Cook the lobsters one after the other, take them out and leave them to cool.

Remove the lobster flesh from the shell, head and claws and slice it neatly.

To make the dressing, place the garlic clove three pinches of salt and the mint leaves in a blender and grind finely. Add the lemon juice, oil and fish stock - one after the other and blend into a marinade.

Wash the cress and arrange it on a serving dish. Slice the turnips and radishes evenly and distribute them around the plate. Arrange the lobster meat on the bed of salad and pour the dressing over it. Leave the salad to stand for another ten minutes.

CALDO GALLEGO

Galician Stockpot

There are two different types of Caldo Gallego. It can be made mainly with vegetables - cabbage, broad beans, potatoes, green beans, pumpkin, turnips and delicate green turnip-tops. Bones, pork belly and fat bacon can also be added to this mixture. The other way is to include various parts of the pig in the Caldo, such as pigs' tails, ears, hocks and trotters, plus a chunk of spicy Galician pepper sausage.

Serves 10	4 white turnips with leaves
	30 g/1 oz pork belly
100 g/3½ oz haricot beans	pepper
1 ham bone	
1 veal bone	**Wine:** a light red wine
salt	such as Valdepeñas,
kg/2½ lb potatoes	Valmansa or Valencia

Soak the beans overnight in cold water. Add the bones and the beans to a large pot with 1½ litres/2½ pints of water, and bring to the boil. Reduce the heat so the liquid simmers. Dice the potatoes and turnips. Reserve the turnip leaves. When the beans are half-cooked (about 1 hour) remove the bones and add the potatoes and turnips. Reduce the heat to a bare simmer. Continue to cook until the vegetables are soft, about 1 hour. Meanwhile, blanch the turnip leaves for a few minutes in salted water. Drain them and add them with the pork belly to the soup. Simmer for another 20 minutes before serving.

RAPE A LA GALLEGA

Monkfish with Potatoes and Garlic Sauce

1 kg/2 lb cooked
monkfish
Salt
2-3 onions
10-12 bay leaves
750 g/1½ lb potatoes
250 ml/8 fl oz oil
2 cloves garlic

½ teaspoon paprika
Pinch of Cayenne or chilli
pepper
Dash of wine vinegar

Wine: a robust, dry white
wine such as Rioja or La
Mancha

Wash the fish, cut it into thick slices and season with salt.
Slice 1 onion in half and reserve half for the garlic sauce.
Reserve one bay leaf. Slice the remaining onions into
rings. Peel the potatoes and put them in a large pot with a
little salt water. Simmer gently until almost cooked. Add
the sliced fish, the onion rings and the bay leaves. Cover
the pot and simmer gently for another 5 minutes.
Meanwhile, prepare the garlic sauce. Peel the garlic, chop
it finely and chop the reserved onion. Heat the oil in a
frying-pan. Fry the onion and garlic until golden brown
with the reserved bay leaf. Remove the pan from the heat
and let the liquid cool. Then season with the paprika and
Cayenne and the vinegar. Drain the fish and potatoes,
arrange them on a serving dish and pour the garlic sauce
over them.

MEJILLONES AL VINO BLANCO

Mussels in White Wine Sauce

Serves 6

3.2 kg/7 lb mussels
½ tablespoon salt
3 garlic cloves
1 bunch of parsley

1 glass (125 ml/4 fl oz)
dry white wine

Wine: a dry white wine.
The best wine in which to cook
the mussels would be something
like Penedès or Cava

Scrub the beards from the mussels and wash them
thoroughly. Discard any which are already open. Bring
375 ml/12 fl oz water to the boil with the salt in a large,
lidded saucepan. Add the mussels and cover the pot
tightly. Steam the mussels for 3 - 8 minutes, depending on
their size, over fairly high heat, until they are all open.
Discard any which have not opened. Strain the cooking
liquid from the mussels through a fine sieve into a bowl
and reserve it for the sauce.
Peel the garlic and chop it finely. Wash the parsley, shake it
dry and chop it finely. Heat the oil in a sauté pan. Fry the
garlic and parsley until they are glazed. Add the wine and
mussel cooking liquid and boil for a further 5 minutes,
stirring frequently. Add the mussels and cook for a few
more minutes. Arrange the mussels in bowls, pour the
cooking liquid over them and serve hot.

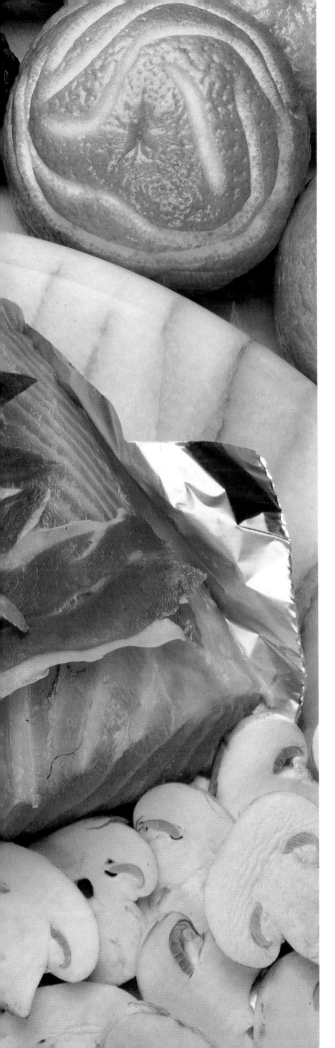

SALMON A NOSO ESTILO

Galician Salmon

Serves 6

1. 4 kg/3 lb filleted salmon
150 g/5 oz butter, softened
300 g/10 oz mushrooms
125 ml/4 fl oz dry sherry (fino)
Few drops Tabasco sauce
1 orange, juice squeezed

Salt
6 slices of Serrano(or prosciutto) ham

Wine: the finest dry white wine you can find, such as Albariño or Rueda

Wash the salmon and slice it into 6 large portions of similar size. Thickly butter 6 large pieces of aluminium foil on one side , leaving an ungreased border round the edge . Sprinkle the salmon pieces with salt and lay them on the buttered foil. Wash mushrooms and trim the stalks. Slice thinly and arrange on the salmon slices. Sprinkle with the sherry, Tabasco sauce, orange juice and salt. Arrange a slice of ham on each piece of salmon.
Fold up the foil into parcels, so as to ensure any liquid will not leak out during cooking and lay them on an baking sheet. Place the tray in the middle of the oven preheated to 200°C/400°F/Gas Mark 6 and bake for 25 minutes. Cut open the foil packets and serve the salmon in the foil.

REO CON ALMEJAS

Sea-trout with Clams

Sea trout are caught in the "rías", funnel-shaped estuaries in north-western Spain.

1 sea-trout, weighing about 1 kg/2½ lb
1 tablespoon of butter
4 tablespoons of oil
2 cloves of garlic
Salt

2 glasses of Albarino wine
1 kg/2 lb clams
1 bunch of parsley

Wine: a robust, dry white wine e.g. Valdepeñas or La Mancha

Ask the fishmonger to skin and bone the trout. Cut the fish into 4 pieces. Rinse the scallops and pat them dry. Heat the butter and oil in a frying-pan and fry the sea-trout lightly on both sides until the flesh is no longer translucent. Peel and finely chop the garlic and add it to the pan along with 2 pinches of salt, the clams and the wine. Cook on a low heat, until the clams have opened. Garnish with chopped parsley before serving.

VIERAS CON COL

Scallops with White Cabbage

16 raw scallops, with coral	Salt
1 kg/2 lb white cabbage	Pepper
250 g/8 oz butter	1 bunch of parsley
60 g/2 oz shallots	
60 ml/2 fl oz dry white wine	**Wine:** a young, slightly-
1 tablespoon olive oil	sparkling white wine

Remove the scallops from the half-shell, wash them and dry them on absorbent kitchen paper. Cut the cabbage in four, discard the stem and wash. the leaves. Shred the cabbage finely and place it in a sauté pan with a lid. Lightly salt it, add 100g/3½ oz of the butter and cover the pan. Fry lightly, stirring and shaking the pan from time to time to prevent sticking. Salt to taste. Peel and chop the shallots. Put them in a small saucepan and cook them on a low heat with the white wine, until they are softened, about 5 minutes. Add the rest of the butter and simmer, covered, on a very low heat for 10-15 minutes. Remove the saucepan from the heat and season with salt and pepper. Cover and keep warm. Heat the grill. Brush the scallops with the oil, so that they do not stick and lay them on a grill rack. Place them under a preheated, hot grill. After 2 minutes carefully turn them over and grill for another 2 minutes. Turn off the grill and keep warm. Preheat the oven to 230°C/450°F/Gas Mark 8.

Arrange the cabbage on 4 ovenproof dishes and place 4 grilled scallops on each dish. Place the dishes in the oven for 1 minute. To serve, garnish with sprigs of parsley and pour some of the shallot butter over the scallops, serving the rest separately.

EMPANADA GALLEGA

Scallop Pie

These pies are made with from a plain bread dough

Serves 8	36 scallops, off the shell
	1 egg, beaten with 2
250 ml/8 fl oz milk	teaspoons water
15 g/½ oz fresh yeast or	2 bay leaves
1 packet dried yeast	5 onions
100 g/3½ oz softened	3 green peppers
butter	3 red peppers
1 teaspoon salt	½ teaspoon ground
1. 2 kg/1½ lb flour	saffron
4 eggs	
125 ml/4 fl oz oil	**Wine:** a light red wine,
2 garlic cloves, peeled	such as Navarra or
2 tomatoes	Ampurdán

Warm the milk with 250 ml/8 fl oz water and add the yeast. Leave, lightly covered, in a warm place until it is foaming. In a bowl, combine the yeast mixture with the butter and salt and mix well. Then fold in the flour and eggs and work into a smooth dough. Cover the bowl with a damp cloth and leave to rise for 30 minutes.

Meanwhile prepare the filling. Coarsely chop the garlic. Heat the oil, add the garlic and the bay leaf and them on medium heat until golden brown. Finely chop the onions and peppers, add them to the pan and brown for a further 20 minutes. Then chop the tomatoes. Add them to the vegetables in the frying-pan and season with salt and saffron. Continue to cook for a few more minutes.

Preheat the oven to 250°C/500°F/Gas Mark 10. Divide the dough into two equal-sized pieces. On a floured board, roll out one piece of dough into a circle about 8 cm/12" in diameter and lay it on a greased baking sheet. Arrange the filling and scallops on top, leaving a 2.5-cm/1-inch border. Roll out the second piece to dough to the same size and lay it on top. Seal the top and bottom pieces of dough together firmly round the edges. Raise the edge slightly and press it with the tines of a fork. Brush with the beaten egg and bake for about 15 minutes.

LACÓN CON GRELOS

Pork Shoulder with Turnip Tops

Lacón is heavily-salted and smoked shoulder of pork which is soaked for 24 hours before cooking. *Grelos* are the young leaves of the turnip which are harvested as soon as they germinate. They can occasionally be found in quantity, but if they are unavailable, use half the quantity of spinach or sorrel and make up the rest with young turnip roots. Butchers in neighbourhoods with a large Caribbean population will usually stock these pickled cuts of pork. This traditional dish was formerly eaten by everyone in the winter months, between Martinmass in November and Mardi Gras in February.

Serves 6

1 kg/2 lb salted and
 smoked shoulder
 of pork
240g/8 oz pickled
 pigs 'ear
250 g/8 oz pickled
pigs' cheek

1. 5 kg/4 lb turnip leaves
600 g/1½ lb chorizo
sausage
12 medium-sized
potatoes, peeled

Wine: a robust red wine
such as Priorato or Ribera
del Duero

Soak the smoked and pickled shoulder ears and cheeks for 24 hours. Scrape and clean them with a knife under running water, then cook for about 90 minutes or until tender in a large saucepan in plenty of water. Remove the meat from the pot and chop it into small pieces. Reserve it in a bowl with some of the stock. Reserve the rest of the stock in the saucepan.

Wash the turnip leaves, chop them into small pieces and cook for 5 minutes in boiling salted water. Drain and rinse the leaves and drain thoroughly. Add them to the saucepan containing the cooking liquid, along with the chorizo and potatoes. Season with salt and simmer on a low heat until the vegetables are tender. Remove them from the heat, cover the pan and leave to stand for 30 minutes.

Pour the stock into a gravy-boat. Arrange the turnip leaves on a large serving dish and place the pieces of pork in the centre, with the sliced sausage and potatoes arranged decoratively across and around the dish. The meat can also be served separately .

CONEJO CON CASTANAS

Rabbit with Chestnuts

Sweet chestnuts were once an important part of the Galician diet. They are delicious when served with wild or domesticated rabbit.

Serves 6

500g/1¼ lb raw sweet
 chestnuts,
 in their shells
2-3 tablespoons oil
2 oven-ready rabbits
2 garlic cloves, peeled
250g/8 oz raw ham
1 onion
2 carrots
A few strands saffron
60 ml/2 fl oz brandy
60 ml/2 fl oz dry sherry

15g/½ oz butter
2 tablespoons flour
1 tablespoon cornflour
 mixed with 2 tablespoons
 water (optional)
Salt

Wine: a red wine "*de
reserva*" (matured for at
least 3 years, one of which
in an oak barrel) such as
the Rioja or Ribera del
Duero.

Slit the unshelled chestnuts with a pointed knife and cook them in boiling water for 5 minutes. Remove the shell and the inner skin. Then cook for a further 30-40 minutes covered in salted water.

Cut each rabbit into three pieces. Heat the oil in a casserole and fry the rabbit pieces with a garlic clove until golden brown. Chop the ham into small pieces. Peel and chop the onions and carrots and add them with the ham, saffron strands and the other clove of garlic. Melt the butter in a small saucepan on a low heat and stir the flour into it. Cook for 2 minutes, then add 125 ml/4 fl oz water and cook, stirring continuously. Add the brandy and the sherry, stir for a few minutes more, then pour the sauce into the casserole. If you want the sauce to be thicker, add cornflour mixture. Season with salt, cover, and simmer for another 40 minutes. Serve with the chestnuts.

FILLOAS

Galician Pancakes

For the pancake batter:
500 ml/16 fl oz milk
225g/7½ oz flour
6 eggs
60g/2 oz butter,
 melted
1 lemon, rind grated
Oil for frying
For the filling:
6 egg yolks

100g/3½ oz sugar
60 g/2 oz flour
250 ml/8 fl oz milk
1 cinnamon stick
½ lemon, rind grated
Castor sugar and ground
cinnamon, for sprinkling

Wine: a strong (up to
23°) sweet dessert wine

or a sparkling Rosé
such as Jerez Oloroso

To make the batter, whisk the milk. gradually adding the flour, melted butter and grated lemon rind. Whisk continuously so that no lumps form. Cover the mixture with a damp cloth and leave it to stand for 30 minutes. Pour a little oil into a non-stick frying-pan, heat until the oil is smoking and add about an eighth of the batter, tipping the pan so that it covers the bottom. Cook until lightly browned, then flip the pancake and cook on the other side. Lay the pancake on absorbent paper while you make the rest of the pancakes with the remaining oil and batter.

To make the cream filling, beat the egg yolks and sugar in a saucepan over a low heat until frothy. Mix the flour with 3 tablespoons of the milk in a bowl. Bring the rest of the milk gradually to the boil with the cinnamon stick and the grated lemon peel. Quickly stir in the flour mixture into the boiling milk and bring to the boil once more. Remove from heat and strain the milk through a sieve into saucepan containing the egg and sugar mixture. Use an egg-beater or whisk to beat the mixture into a creamy consistency over low heat. Use this mixture to fill pancakes and sprinkle them with sugar and ground cinnamon. Serve with lemon wedges.

ASTURIAS AND CANTABRIA

Asturias and Cantabria lie between the Basque country and the Bay of Biscay. The landscapes of these two provinces are probably the most beautiful in Spain. The Asturian coastline stretches for 300 kilometres and is lined with quiet coves, sandy beaches and rugged cliffs. The Cantabrian coastline has long stretches of beach which are popular with Spaniards who live in those parts of the country where it is unmercifully hot in the summer. Inland, the countryside is rich and green, separated from the rest of Spain by the Cantabrian Mountains.

The regional cuisines of these provinces are in many ways very similar, despite their different political and social history.

One of Asturias's most popular dishes is Fabada, *a rich soup made with white beans, onions, pigs trotters, pork fat, pigs blood and pepper sausage. For those who enjoy shellfish, there is also a variation of Fabada made with clams. Asturian cuisine specializes mainly in fish dishes, such as* Caldereta de Pescado, *a colourful mixture of Cantabrian fish which is just as popular as Fabada. Beef, ox tripe and various Asturian sausages, whose ingredients include blood, chilli pepper, black pepper and other spices are amongst the delicacies on offer inland. The local Asturian drink is* Sidra - apple cider. *This light, sparkling version is not only good to drink but is used in cooking.* Merluza a la sidra *(Hake in cider) is an excellent main course after the* fabada.

Cantabria also has delicious fish dishes, for example sardinas en cazuela de Laredo (*Laredo-style sardines*) and rabas Santander (*Squid à la Santander*). *The recipes for both these dishes date back to the Middle Ages. In the Cantabrian countryside tripe is very popular and features in* callos a la montanesa, *in which it is cooked with red peppers and a wine sauce. Other inland favourites are* Pollo Campurriano (*Chicken with rice and peppers*) *and* Habas a la manera del país (*broad beans with ham and onions*).

Cantabria, unlike many other regions, has been cooking with butter for a long time. This is hardly surprising, in view of the region's large herds of cattle and dairy economy. Dairy foods are popular, including a delicious rice dish called arroz a la santanderina, *which also contains fresh salmon, milk and butter.*

Pages 30/31:
Typical Cantabrian
fishing village.

Top left: The cider
will really foam if is
poured from a
great height.

Top right: Sotres in
the Valley of Las
Monetas in
Cantabria.

Below: Corn cobs
hung out to dry in a
sheltered spot on a
house front are
typically seen in
Asturias.

Fish from the Atlantic
Cheese from the Mountains

The Cantabrian Mountains of Cantabria sharply divides Asturias from León and Old Castile , giving it a completely different climate from inland and southern Spain. The influence of the turbulent waters of the Bay of Biscay is also strong, especially at the time of the autumn storms and the resulting high tides. It is hardly surprising therefore that the inhabitants of Asturias and Cantabria are of a serious rather introverted temperament. They are not as light-hearted as their fellow Mediterranean countrymen. Their close ties with the elements of earth and water are reflected in their native cuisines.

The culinary roots of both these regions are nurtured on the one hand by the fishermen and hunters and on the other by the farmers and the cattle ranchers. The fish harvest of the Atlantic and Cantabrian seas has strongly influenced the Spanish inland style of cooking. For hundreds of years, fish could only be sent to León, Castile, La Rioja or Navarre in the cool season. They were transported on the backs of mules. Today, it is easy to supply fish to the interior all year round, thanks to modern refrigerated transport.

Hake is the king of fish in northern Spain, and it is caught both by coarse fishermen with rods and in nets. Hake is the predominant fish in the traditional dishes of Asturias, Cantabria and the Basque country. It is also highly prized inland, particularly in Burgos, where it is coated in egg and breadcrumbs and fried in the finest oil. Other tasty ways of preparing hake include *merluza en salsa verde* (Hake in a garlic-and-parsley sauce) *merluza en salsa roja* (Hake with onions, paprika, garlic and wine), or *merluza al pil pil*, a predominantly Basque method of preparation, in which the hake is simmered in oil and garlic.

However hake is not the only prized fish from the Cantabrian seas. These northernmost regions have produced many other fish dishes, using the many varieties harvested from the depths of the ocean, including sea-bream, anchovies, flounder, albacore and white tuna, sardines and whitebait, halibut, dogfish (huss), turbot, squid, crabs, prawns and shrimps. Asturias and Cantabrians have more delicious fish dishes than any other part of the Iberian peninsula.There is also evidence of French influence from the seafarers of Brittany and Normandy .

Asturias is not only a region blessed with fine fish; the lush meadows of its great mountain ranges produce superb cheeses. Even the names of the cheeses melt on the tongue;. There is the cow's milk cheese from Oviedo called *Afuega el Pitu* and the delicious-sounding cheese *Gamoneda*, which can be made from the milk of cows, goats or ewes. Gamoneda is as popular a cheese as *Queso de Calabrés*, a strong, blue-veined cheese reminiscent of Roquefort or Stilton and matured in the same way. The strong taste of Calabres cheese is at its best when it has been allowed to mature for six months. The secret of this "holy" cheese was spirited away by French monks who passed through Asturias s on a pilgrimage to Santiago de Compostela in the 17th century and exported it over the Pyrenees.

In these regions, whether one is eating a fish dish, *fabada* the local rich soup or a cheese such as *Queso de Beyos*, the popular local cider is the ideal complement. This Asturian national drink is related to that of the nearby French provinces of Normandy and Brittany. The two areas have much in common, and their inhabitants have long enjoyed a close relationship, through their seafaring. If you ever visit Asturias, find a bar that serves *sidra* and watch the way the waiters pour the lightly-fermented apple nectar into glasses. They use a swinging motion, producing in an arc-shaped jet from the bottle to the glass from quite some distance. All though this reflects the Spanish penchant for the theatrical, it also has a practical purpose, since it makes the cider foam as it bounces off the inside of the glass. One could say that *sidra* embodies the qualities and spirit of the northern Spanish coast, in that it is beautifully rough and topped with foam.

If you want to experience the impressive might of the Bay of Biscay's storms, it is best to do so from the safety of the ports. The battered fishing boats and torn fishing nets ought to be warning enough that the high seas of the Atlantic are not to be treated lightly.

Page 34: The net is hauled in from the stern of the vessel.

Left: The best, freshly-caught fish are available in the harbour market.

Below left: The fish are sorted onboard before the boat reaches port.

Below: This fine catch has been hauled in by a trawler net.

FABADA ASTURIANA

Asturian Bean Stew

The name "Fabada" is derived from *fabe*, the large Asturian white bean. The recipe for Asturian bean stew is an ancient one. As in the French dish "cassoulet", the basic ingredient is dried white beans. Nowadays, The other main ingredient in the Fabada is pork, but other meat can be included, such as hare, quail or even clams, depending on what is available. The combination of dried beans and pork is a typical basic dish of the Iberian peninsula.

The following recipe uses *longaniza*, an oven-cured pork sausage, which is a speciality of Asturias. If not available, use any spicy cured pork sausage. Fresh haricot beans. If you use dried haricot beans, instead of blanching them for 5 minutes, use 500g/1½ lb and soak them overnight.

Serves 6

1 kg/2 lb dried, salted pork shoulder or ham
500g/1½ lb smoked bacon
1 pickled pigs' ear
1 pickled pigs' trotter
1 kg/2 lb fresh haricot beans
1 garlic clove

1 bay leaf
250g/9 oz morcilla (blood sausage)
3 longanizas (spicy smoked pork sausages)
Salt

Wine: a robust red wine such as Jumilla or Campo de Borja

Soak the salt and pickled pork for 12 hours, changing the water at least once. Slice the meat into bite-sized pieces and place it in a pot,. Add water to cover, cover with a lid on the pan and simmer on a low heat. When the meat has been cooking for 1 hour, put the beans into a separate pot, add water to cover and boil briskly for 5 minutes. Drain and discard the cooking water. Add the beans to the pot with the meat along with the garlic and the bay leaf. Continue to simmer over a low heat for another hour. Then add the blood sausage and the spicy sausages. Season with salt and cook until the beans reach a soft thick consistency.

MERLUZA A LA SIDRA

Hake in Cider Sauce

3 large onions
3 cloves of garlic
500 g/1½ lb tomatoes
¼ teaspoon paprika
125 ml/4 fl oz dry cider
12 clams
1.5 kg/3 lb 5 oz middle
cut of hake
Salt

200 g/7 oz flour
500 ml/16 fl oz oil
500 g/1 lb potatoes

Wine: *Sidra* if possible,
Asturias produces
excellent cider, otherwise
any slightly sparkling good
dry cider.

Cut the hake into thick slices, lightly salt them and coat in
the flour. Peel the potatoes and cut them into thin slices.
Heat half the oil and fry the fish steaks on both sides in
half the oil. Reserve them in a warm place on a serving
dish. Add the potatoes to the oil in the pan and sauté until
golden brown. Arrange the potatoes in an ovenproof dish
and lay the fish slices on top. Peel, finely chop and fry the
onions and garlic until lightly browned in the remaining
oil in another saucepan. Add the tomatoes and paprika
and stir together thoroughly. Add the cider and bring the
sauce to the boil on a high heat. Season with salt. Preheat
the oven to 200°C/400°F/Gas Mark 6. Then strain the
sauce through a sieve over the potatoes and fish. Garnish
with the clams and bake in the oven for 10 minutes or
until piping hot.

TRONCO DE MERLUZA

Hake with Clams

1. 4 kg/3 lb hake,
middle cut
Salt
3 tablespoons flour
Oil
250 ml/8 fl oz fish stock
600 g/1½ lb clams, well
washed

2 cloves garlic, peeled
100 g/3½ oz parsley,
chopped

Wine: a full-bodied, dry
white wine such as Alella
or Costers del Segre

Slice the fish into four steaks, season it with salt, coat in
flour and shallow-fry in oil on medium heat. Add the fish
stock and cook for 2 minutes. Add the clams, the garlic
and chopped parsley. As soon as the clams open, stir in
the flour to thicken the liquid. Simmer on a low heat for a
few more minutes until it is ready to serve.

CALDARETA ASTURIANA

Asturias Fish Stew

1 kg/2 lb saltwater fish with
lean, firm flesh such as red
perch or sea bass, gutted
500 g/1½ lb mussels or clams
8 large shrimps
125 ml/4 fl oz oil
1 onion
1 tablespoon paprika
Salt
1 large sweet red pepper
100 g/3½ oz parsley
12 black peppercorns
125 ml/4 fl oz dry
sherry (fino)
½ teaspoon nutmeg
½ small chilli pepper

Wine: a dry white
wine such as
Valdeorras or
Penedès

Wash the fish and shellfish and
put them in a flameproof dish. Pour
the oil over. them Peel and chop the
onions and add them along with the
paprika and ½ teaspoon of salt. Stir thoroughly

and fry until the shells open. Add 125-250 ml/4-8 fl oz water and bring to the boil. Wash, seed and finely chop the sweet red pepper and the chilli. pepper. Coarsely chop the parsley. Add these ingredients along with the peppercorns, sherry and nutmeg to the stew. Cover and simmer on a low heat for 20 minutes.

SARDINAS EN CAZUELA

Sardines in a Clay Pot

1 kg/2 lb sardines
Salt
200 ml/7 fl oz oil
300 g/10 oz onions
1 bay leaf
1 tablespoon paprika

Wine: a full-bodied white wine or a rosé, such as one from Rioja or Alicante.

Scale the sardines, cut off their heads, gut, wash and salt them. Heat the oil in a large flameproof earthenware pot with a lid . Peel and slice the onions, add them to the pot with the paprika and bay leaf and fry lightly. Bring 125 ml/4 fl oz water to the boil in a saucepan and allow the sardines to stew in their own juice for a while. Then heap the fish in the earthenware pot. Cover the pot tightly and simmer on a low heat until the fish are cooked, about 20 minutes, stirring from time to time, so the sardines do not stick to the bottom of the pot.

RABAS EN SALSA VERDE

Squid in green sauce

1 kg/2 lb squid
200 ml/7 fl oz oil
1 sprig of parsley
2 slices of toasted white bread, crusts removed
125 ml/4 fl oz white wine
Salt

Wine: a full-bodied, dry white wine such as Rueda or Tarragona

Wash the squid in hot water. Discard the ink sac and slice the body and tentacles into strips. Heat the oil in a saucepan and fry the squid for ten minutes, leaving the pan uncovered, so that the liquid can evaporate. Here is an amazing trick. To stop the squid becoming rubbery, add a cork to it whilst it is frying and remove and discard it when the juice has dried out.
Chop the parsley and dice the toast into croutons. Sprinkle both over the squid Sprinkle with the white wine, cover the pan and cook over a low heat. Season with salt and add a little more wine or some water when it dries out. Cook until the squid are tender, about 15 minutes.

FARIÑES

Corn Pudding

12 tablespoons yellow cornmeal
Salt
Sugar or honey

Wine: a dessert wine (Rosado from Alicante or amontillado sherry)

Pour 600 ml/1 pint of very cold water into a large deep pot. on the stove, but do not heat it. Pour the cornmeal into the pot quickly, stirring continuously with a long wooden stick or spoon so that no lumps form. Then heat the mixture and continue stirring. Season generously with salt and continue to cook, stirring constantly, until the mixture thickens. Serve with hot milk and sugar.

ESTOFADO DE BUEY

Stewed Beef

The meat normally cooked this way is ox or bull, which is tough but well-flavoured and needs long, slow cooking. It is an excellent way to use cheap, lean cuts of beef.

50 g/2 oz pork dripping or lard	Mixed herbs or
400 g/13 oz beef shin	bouquet garni
500 g/1½ lb onions	120 g/4 oz carrots
120 g/4 oz smoked bacon	120 g/4 oz turnips
500 g/1½ lb knuckle of veal	120g/4 oz parsnips
100 g/3½ oz parsley	250 ml/8 fl oz red wine
Freshly-ground black pepper	250 ml/8 fl oz vinegar
Salt	

Heat the dripping or lard in a large saucepan, add the shin of beef and brown all over. Peel the onions, slice them into rings and dice the bacon. Clean the carrots, turnips and parsnips and chop them coarsely. Chop the parsley finely. Add the onion rings, bacon cubes, the knuckle of veal, the rest of the vegetables, salt, pepper, the parsley and the bouquet garni to the saucepan. Cook, uncovered on a low heat until all the liquid has evaporated. Now add the wine and vinegar, increase the heat and cook until all the liquid has boiled away. Add 500 ml/16 fl oz water. Cover and simmer on a lower heat for another 3 hours.

Place the meat in the middle of a large shallow serving dish, surround with vegetables and pour the cooking juices over it.

THE BASQUE
COUNTRY

*U*nadulterated traditional cooking is the hallmark of the Basque kitchen. Although here too, a nueva cocina vasca has been in existence for some 20 years, in most cases this is simply a development of old recipes, whilst remaining true to traditional principles.

*T*he Basque country has a long coastline and a long fishing tradition. As a result, Basque cuisine is based mainly on fish dishes. Fish and salted fish such as bacalao (salt cod) may be prepared in innumerable ways. Two of the most interesting inventions in the art of Basque fish preparation are marmitako, essentially consisting of fresh tuna and potatoes and toro, a hearty stew. Other culinary delights include lomos de merluza (hake fillets), almejas a la marinara (clams in onion, garlic and wine sauce), chipirones en su tinta (small squid cooked in their own ink), angulas a la vasca (eel cooked in oil and garlic), la merluza en salsa verde (hake in herb sauce), el besugo de Bermeo (Sea bream, caught in the waters around the fishing village of Bermeo) and el txangurro relleno (stuffed spider-crab).

*T*he Basques are unsurpassed in their preparation of bacalao, dried salt cod, whether it be al pil pil (slowly stewed in olive oil and garlic), al ajoarriero (with onions, garlic, parsley and

Overleaf: San Sebastian in the
Basque province.

Right: Typical farmhouses in
evergreen Basque country.

a pinch ofchilli), a la vizcaína *(in a spicy onion, garlic and paprika sauce) or* al Club Ranero *(according to the recipe of the famous Basque gastronomic society). Different cooking techniques have been developed for Atlantic fish, since they have a different flavour and character to the fish of the Mediterranean,*

T*he Basque kitchen also produces some excellent meat dishes, such as the large ox or calf steaks known as* villagodios, *named after a famous breed of fighting bull. Other dishes include* tripacallos a la viscaína, *(Biscay-style tripe),* cordonices con hoja de parra *(quails with vine leaves),* ganso adobado *(preserved goose, somewhat similar to the "confit d'oie" from Gascony in France),* cordero en salsa picante *(lamb in spicy sauce), the edible fungus dish* perechico *from Vitoria prepared in an earthenware pot and* becada con nabos *(woodcock with turnips).*

C*akes and desserts include* bizcochos rellenos de Vergara *or* bizcochos de Mendaro, *biscuits baked in the style of* Vergara or Mendaro. *There are also the almond slices from Tolosa,* almendrados de Tolosa. *The high point of the Basque dessert menu is* arroz con leche, *the famous rice pudding, which is actually not originally a Basque dish but one whose preparation has been brought to perfection by the Basques.*

Picture left: "The Wind Flows" by the artists of Chillida near San Sebastian.

Right: The sheep from the plains play an important part in Basque cuisine.

Bacalao - Stockfish or Dried Cod

Lamb, ewes' milk cheeses and fish: these seemingly disparate ingredients constitute the backbone of the Basque kitchen. They aptly reflect the nature of the changing landscape and the economy balanced between land and sea. If you find yourself in the Basque Country in the autumn, you may be fortunate enough to come across a Basque feast, a very jolly affair. These banquets, which are known as *txarribodas* or *sartenek,* capture the authentic flavour of the Basque Country. As in days gone by, away from the industrial centres, the shepherds still drive their large herds of sheep through the sparsely populated Basque mountains. It is therefore hardly surprising that tender lamb dishes and tasty ewes' milk cheeses, often flavoured with rosemary and thyme, are an essential part of the menu.

The same is true of Basque fish dishes, which use both saltwater fish from the Bay of Biscay, and trout from the mountain streams.

The ridged mountain chain, the green valleys and fields, the apple orchards and corn fields all stretch out towards the Basque coast, where the climate is mild and popular with summer visitors.

The Basque people live in both Spain and over the border in France. They call their land *Euskadi* and their language *Euskera,. Bacalao,* however, is neither a Basque word nor is it an exclusively Basque dish. Anyone asking for *bacalao* will be understood along the whole northern coastline of the Basque country, Asturias, Galicia and even northern Portugal.

Recipes for stockfish, dried salt fish, known in Spain as bacalao belong to the traditional repertoire of Spanish cuisine and every region has developed its own particular method of preparing this fish. It is even popular in south-western France and in Portugal. However the Basques are noted for their expertise in this area. This technique of preserving fish was probably devised by the whalers of days gone by on their long journeys on the high seas. Consequently the dried cod recipes in the provinces bordering the Bay of Biscay have a long history.

Dried cod was originally a staple dish in times of fasting and from the 15th century until the middle of this century was considered to be highly nutritious. Since then, the price of *bacalao* has risen continuously as demand increased, so turning this tasty dish into an expensive delicacy.

It is almost impossible to count all the ways in which *bacalao* can be prepared, there is supposedly a different recipe for every day of the year. A classic method involves cooking it in fresh water and adding sliced red and green peppers, previously sweated in butter, and boiled sliced potatoes. Layers of fish, peppers, tomatoes and potatoes are arranged in an earthenware pot and covered in a sauce made with melted butter, flour, fish stock and spices. The pot is baked without a lid until the top is lightly browned and crispy. This a delicious, dish, is the classic *bacalao al pil pil,* which should be accompanied by red or white dry Spanish wine.

The Basque country still has an active tradition of gastronomic societies which in the villages double as men's clubs. The societies value fine cooking and the exchange of recipes although other topics for discussion such as politics, sport and business. are also on the agenda at regular club meetings One might well wonder how many deals have been made using *bacalao* as the the intermediary!

Left and right: Bacalao is sold unpackaged from both market stalls and the grocers' shops.

typical of Basque cooking. The sauce should have a rather liquid consistency. This means that the cooking juices from the cod and the oil are combined by standing over the pan and constantly stirring the mixture until it becomes a delicious velvety, cream-coloured, aromatic sauce.

600 g /1½ lb dried cod
6 garlic cloves
250 ml/8 fl oz olive oil
1 bunch of parsley, chopped

Wine: a light Rosé or red wine from Campo de Borja or Tarragona

Cut the cod into pieces and soak it for 24 hours. Change the water at least twice.
Heat the oil in a shallow flameproof earthenware pot or enamelled flameproof casserole and add the whole, peeled garlic cloves, along with the chopped parsley. Sauté until golden brown. Remove the pot from the heat and allow to cool. Remove the garlic cloves from the oil and reserve them. Lay the cod, skin side down, in the pot. Slowly cook it over a low heat. so that the liquid thickens into a creamy sauce. Stir frequently, and do not allow the sauce to come to the boil. Garnish the dish with the reserved garlic cloves before serving.

LA PURRUSALDA

Cod with Leek and Potatoes

480 g /1 lb dried cod
90 ml/3 fl oz oil
2 garlic cloves, peeled
600 g /1½ lb potatoes
480 g /1 lb leeks
1 bay leaf

½ teaspoon paprika
Salt
Pepper

Wine: a young red wine or Rosé

Soak the cod in very cold water for 24 hours, changing the water at least twice. Drain the fish thoroughly, place it in a stew-pan and add 500 ml/16 fl oz water. Boil for 5 minutes. Remove the pan from the heat and leave the fish standing in the cooking liquid for 10 minutes. Strain off the fish stock into a bowl. Skin and bone the cod and cut it into small pieces.
Heat the oil in a deep frying-pan and fry the peeled garlic cloves until golden brown. Peel and dice the potatoes. Wash the leeks and slice them into rings. Add the potatoes and leeks to the garlic in the pan and fry for a few minutes. Then add the cod and season with paprika. Pour the fish stock into the pan, add salt and pepper to taste and cook for another half an hour. Serve piping hot.

BACALAO AL PIL PIL

Dried Cod in Garlic Sauce

The secret behind the preparation of this dried cod dish is in the quality of the sauce. The technique employed is

ALMEJAS A LA MARINERA

Clams in White Wine

White pepper
100 g/3½ oz parsley
Salt
1. 2 kg/2½ lb clams
100 ml/3½ fl oz olive oil
2 garlic cloves
1 onion

1 table spoon flour
125 ml/4 fl oz dry white wine

Wine: a full-bodied white wine such as an Alella from La Mancha

Wash the clams thoroughly and discard any shells which have already opened. Heat the olive oil in a flameproof casserole with a lid. Peel and finely chop the onions and garlic and fry them gently in the oil until the onions are transparent. Sprinkle with flour, let the liquid thicken a little and then add the wine and water. Increase the heat and bring the liquid to the boil. Now add the clams and cover the pan tightly. After 5 minutes or so the clams should have opened; discard any which are still closed. Remove the pot from the heat and stir the clams several times. Season with salt and white pepper. Sprinkle generously with chopped parsley and serve.

CHIPIRONES EN SU TINTA

Squid in their Own Ink

In this recipe, the sauce is made by using the ink from the squid. The dish is believed by many to have originated from the Far East. because the Chinese and Japanese have always been masters in the preparation of dishes with ingredients, which in their raw state are poisonous, but which are safe when cooked, such as the ink in squid. However, the Oriental origins of this Basque dish have not been proven. In any case, this is considered to be a typical Basque speciality which is usually served with rice.

1 kg/2 lb small, whole squid
250 g /8 oz flour
200 ml/6 fl oz olive oil

2 medium-sized onions
2 cloves garlic
100 g /3½ oz ham
2 small tomatoes
1 bunch of parsley
125 ml/4 fl oz dry white wine
Enough boiled rice for 4 people

To prepare the squid: carefully separate the ink sacs with a knife, taking care to prevent them bursting. Collect them in a small bowl. Wash the squid thoroughly, discard the "beak", turn it inside out and stuff the tentacles inside the body . Close the opening with toothpicks. Sprinkle the squid, with salt and dust them lightly with flour. Heat the oil in a frying-pan and fry the squid until golden brown. Remove the squid and drain them on absorbent kitchen paper. Remove the toothpicks and put the squid in an ovenproof earthenware casserole. Peel and finely chop the onions and garlic. Dice the ham. Wash the tomatoes and parsley, dry thoroughly and chop them finely. Add everything to the casserole dish and simmer on a low heat for about 10 minutes. Meanwhile carefully empty the ink sacs of their ink . Discard the sacs and mix the ink with 125 ml/4 fl oz warm water and the white wine. Strain the mixture through a sieve into the casserole dish, blend thoroughly with the ham-and-tomato sauce and continue to cook on a very low heat until the squid are tender, about 30 minutes. Serve on a bed of rice.

MARMITAKO

Basque Tuna fish Casserole

1 kg/2 lb fresh tuna fish	200 ml/7 fl oz oil
Salt	8 thick slices French bread
1 onion	
4 tomatoes	**Wine:** a full-bodied, dry
4 green peppers	white wine such as a
1 kg/2 lb potatoes	˙Penedès from Albariño

Cut the tuna fish into steaks and sprinkle it with salt. Peel and chop the onions. Steep the tomatoes in boiling water for a few minutes, skin them and roughly chop them. Wash and clean the peppers and slice them into strips. Peel and cube the potatoes. Heat 2 tablespoons of the oil in a casserole dish and add the onions, tomatoes, peppers, potatoes and the tuna fish . Cover the pot and simmer for 20 minutes or until all the ingredients are tender.
Meanwhile fry the slices of bread in the rest of the oil and serve them with the tuna casserole.

MERLUZA EN SALSA VERDE

Hake in Green Sauce

4 thick hake steaks	**Wine:** a full-bodied dry
Salt	white wine such as a
1-2 tablespoons flour	Valdepeñas from Valencia
150 ml/10 fl oz oil	
4 cloves garlic	
1 bunch of parsley	

Season the slices of hake with salt and coat them lightly with flour. Heat the oil in a flameproof casserole dish and fry the fish on both sides. Peel the garlic, wash and dry the parsley and finely chop them both. Put them in a bowl with 1/2 teaspoon of flour and 125 ml/4 fl oz of water and whisk thoroughly with a fork. Pour the sauce over the fish and simmer gently for another 5 minutes, stirring from time to time.

ANGUILAS A LA VASCA

Eel Basque-style

The life story of the eel is a really extraordinary one. The spawning grounds of all the European and American eels in the Atlantic Ocean lie between the Azores and the Bahamas in the area known as the Sargasso Sea. The baby eels, known as elvers ,begin their journey from the Gulf Stream to the north-eastern Atlantic when they are barely 1 millimetre in length. It takes them three years to reach their destination. Although many die on the way, many more survive the long trip. Those which remain in salt water become males, whilst those which make it upstream into the rivers and lakes turn into females. Eels can be cooked in a variety of different ways. Once the food of the poor, nowadays eel is an expensive luxury. Never handle hot chilli peppers with bare hands .

Serves 6	1 hot red chilli pepper
	600 g /1 1/2 lb eel
600 ml/1 pint oil	
3 cloves garlic	**Wine:** a red wine such as
	an Almansa from Alicante

Cut the eel into 6 portions. Peel the garlic and slice it thinly. Heat the oil on a high heat in a large frying pan and fry the garlic until golden brown. Meanwhile, seed the chilli pepper and chop the chilli into small pieces . Add it to the pan along with the eel. As soon as the fish is cooked (a few minutes at most), remove the pan from the heat, place it on a heat-resistant mat and serve.

This "slippery eel" delicacy, is eaten in the Basque country with a hand-carved wooden spoon.

TZANGURRO RELLENO

Stuffed Spider-Crab

Serves 1

1 teaspoon breadcrumbs
1 tablespoon chopped
parsley
1 large and 1 medium-
sized spider crab
½ onion
2 cloves garlic
1 small leek
1 tablespoon olive oil

2 tomatoes
30 g /1 oz butter
Salt
Pepper
60 ml/2 fl oz cognac or dry
sherry (fino)

Wine: a full-bodied white
wine such as an Albariño
from La Mancha.

Combine the breadcrumbs and parsley. Open the crab
bodies and legs with pincers or a sharp knife, remove all
the flesh and chop finely. Scrape out the shell of the large
crab, wash and dry the insides with absorbent kitchen
paper. Peel and finely chop the onion and garlic. Wash,
clean and chop the leek. Heat the oil in a frying-pan and
fry the vegetables until golden brown. Meanwhile steep
the tomatoes for several minutes, then skin. Purée them
by pushing them through a fine sieve. Add the tomato
purée to the vegetables and cook for 2 minutes. Then add
the crabmeat and the butter. Stir and season with salt and
pepper. Add the cognac or sherry, stir and simmer on a
low heat for another 8-10 minutes. Preheat the oven to
200°C/400°F/Gas Mark 6. When the stuffing is ready, fill
the shells on an ovenproof dish. Sprinkle with the
parsley-and-breadcrumb mixture and complete
the garnish with a sprig of parsley in the middle.
Bake until lightly browned, about 10 minutes.

ARROZ CON LECHE

Basque Rice Pudding

500 ml/16 fl oz milk
1 lemon rind
1 cinnamon stick
100 g /3½ oz short-grained or
pudding rice
50 g /2 oz butter
120 g/4 oz sugar
2 egg yolks, beaten
About 1 tablespoon ground cinnamon

Simmer the milk with the lemon peel and cinnamon stick
on a low heat. Just before the rice comes to the boil,
add the milk, cover the pan, and continue to cook
gently on a low heat for about 50 minutes. Then
add the butter and sugar and simmer for a
further 10 minutes. Remove the pan from the
heat and beat in the egg yolks. Sprinkle with
cinnamon and serve.

RIOJA, ARAGÓN, NAVARRA

The culinary traditions of Rioja, Aragón and Navarra have much in common with each other. Sheep-rearing is widespread in all these regions and there is an abundance of vegetables and poultry. The noteworthy dishes of these provinces include Trucha a la Navarra *(trout with raw ham), lamb cutlets cooked in the particular style of Rioja and Navarra,* Cochefrito *(lamb stewed in a an earthenware pot) and most especially Navarran asparagus, which is prized throughout Spain and even beyond.*

A dried, salted cod dish called El bacalao al ajoarreiro *is popular throughout these regions. It is served in a sauce made with garlic, parsley, sweet peppers and bread soaked in wine.*

Overleaf: Paracuellos de Jiloca in Aragón.

Right: Grape picking in Rioja, the most famous wine-growing area in Spain.

Below: Automated wine-bottling plant.

Traditional dishes of Aragón include ternasco, *spit-roasted suckling lamb,* migas a la aragonesa *(fried bacon rashers in tomato sauce), not forgetting the dried ham from the Teruel mountains. There is a variety of sausages such as the oven-cured pork sausage called* longaniza *and* morcilla, *a blood pudding from Aragón. On the whole, the cuisine of Navarra has more variety to offer than that of Aragón. The farm produce of Aragón, however, is of the finest quality, lending a special flavour to the local dishes. The vegetables and pulses are particularly aromatic and tender.*

In Aragón and Rioja, many dishes are cooked al chilindrón, *i.e, in a sauce made with fresh tomatoes, onions and chilli pepper. Chicken is often served in this sauce and the resulting flavour is unmistakable. The cuisine of Rioja is essentially Castilian, although it has also been influenced by those of Aragón and Navarra. It is extremely tasty, yet very simple. Those who have tasted* pochas *(freshly-picked beans, flavoured in a variety of ways) will not forget the experience. Dishes prepared* a la Riojana *include paprika and the local spicy* chorizo *sausage. The* chorizos *of Rioja and Estremadura are the best in Spain.*
An unusual combination popular in this region is a dish of tripe and potatoes eaten with snails. Whatever you eat here, it always goes down best with a glass or two of Rioja wine.

Left: Wine is still matured in oak casks. This is the Bodega Palacios (La Rioja Alavesa).

Below: Houses are closely huddled together to provide shelter from the heat. Jumble of roofs in a typical Aragonese town.

Pimentos and Wine

The red chilli pepper known as *piementón* is a speciality of Rioja, Aragón and Navarre. Tiny red peppers are dried, then chopped and ground into powder. These peppers were brought to Spain in the 17th century by the conquistadors of America. In the past, the flavour was only appreciated locally. Foreign visitors such as the Baron de Bourgogne, who visited Spain in the late 19th century, claimed that *"the Spanish love strong, hot flavours such as pepper, tomato sauce and paprika, which do not merely colour the dishes, they smother them"*.

This attitude has changed dramatically, and today, Spaniards and foreigners alike greatly enjoy the flavour of this ground chilli pepper. Although the plant has been cultivated in Estremadura (to be precise in the *Oega* of Plasencia) and in the Andalusian district of Murcia since the 17th century, it is nevertheless associated with Rioja. It was from Rioja that *pimentón* began its conquest of Spanish kitchens. When it was first used is a mystery. Although it is not mentioned in a Castilian dictionary published in 1726, it must have become popular very soon thereafter . It was in about that time, that the father-in-law of the painter Francisco de Goya, Ramón Bayen, painted a mural in El Escorial depicting the famous *Choricero* or sausage-maker - proof of the early popularity of the *pimentón*, which is an essential ingredient in the sausage.

Since then pimento has enriched the flavour of many a dish, including such favourites as potatoes *a la riojana* , Castilian garlic soup, Galician *ajada*, Majorcan *sobrasada*, the chorizos from Huelva to La Rioja and the sausages of Levante. It also contributes to the unmistakable flavour of *paella valenciana*, being as essential an ingredient as the saffron.

Pimentón is undoubtedly the essential ingredient in many of the dishes of Navarra and Aragón. These include *chilindrón aragonés,* a tomato, onion and pepper sauce,

Below pp. 60-61: The freshly-picked pimentos are dried out in the sun, later to be ground into pepper.

Below: Pimentón, the hot red pepper ground from the small red chillis known as pimentos.

pimientos rellenos riojanos, Rioja-style stuffed peppers and *codornices al pimiento de la ribera Navarra*, partridges with peppers.

Without a shadow of a doubt, if the Spanish conquistadors had not brought back this spice from the Americas, Spanish cuisine would have been rather dull and repetitive. Tomatoes and peppers are undoubtedly the most important flavourings in Spanish cooking.

The most famous wine growing area in Spain was named after a small tributary of the Ebro, the Rio Oja, producing the name Rioja.

The tradition of Riojan wine-making started as a result of the disaster that befell the vine-growers of Bordeaux in the 19th century. Their grapes were afflicted with phylloxera, a devastating disease of the vine, which spread right from Bordeaux as far as the Ebro. The disease became seemed to half at Logroño and Haro, so that a new wine-growing region was started in Rioja. One can taste the shared characteristics of Bordeaux and Rioja wines from the very first sip.

TRUCHAS A LA NAVARRA

Navarra Trout

4 dressed trout, each
weighing about
150-200 g/5-6½ oz
4 slices raw ham,
preferably Spanish ham
60 g/2 oz flour
60 g/2 oz bacon fat or lard
90 ml/3 fl oz olive oil

1 lemon
Salt
Pepper

Wine: a robust, dry
white wine or a Rosé,
such as a Penedès from
Albariño.

Wash the trout and dry it thoroughly with kitchen paper. Wrap a slice of ham around each fish and dust with flour. Melt the bacon fat or lard in a frying-pan. Fry the fish in the fat for about 5 minutes on each side. Arrange the fish in a serving dish. Squeeze the lemon juice over them and season with salt and pepper.

BACALAO AL AJOARRIERO

Muleteer's Cod

The following method of preparing cod is popular throughout Navarre, Rioja and Aragon. It is a very old recipe and is mentioned in Cervantes' *Don Quixote de la Mancha*. Dried cod can be found in shops specialising in Caribbean food.

500 g/1 1/2 lb dried cod (bacalao)
120 g/4 oz flour
200 ml/7 fl oz olive oil
5 garlic cloves
1 bunch of parsley
About 125 ml/4 fl oz dry red wine

1 teaspoon chilli pepper
1 slice of white bread, crusts removed

Wine: a young red wine or a Rosé, perhaps from Jumilla or Navarra

Soak the cod for 24 hours, changing the water at least twice. Discard the water, dry the fish and slice it into pieces of roughly equal size. Discard the black skin and any remaining bones. Coat the fish pieces in flour. Heat the oil in a frying-pan on a fairly high heat and fry the fish until golden-brown. Meanwhile, peel the garlic, wash and dry the parsley and chop both finely. Tear the bread into small pieces and soak it in a little red wine. In a bowl, combine garlic, parsley, and paprika with the bread, and work into a paste. Add this to the cod in the pan, stir well and continue to cook on a high heat for a few minutes. Then reduce the heat, cover the pan and stew for a further 25 minutes.

PIMIENTOS RELLENOS

Stuffed Peppers

Serves 6

360 g/12 oz stewing steak
1 bay leaf
5 black peppercorns
6 large, sweet red peppers
3 onions
2 garlic cloves
1 bunch of parsley
2 slices white bread,
crusts removed
30 g/1 oz butter

200 g/7 oz minced beef or
lamb
1 tablespoon dried thyme
Salt
Pepper
Oil to grease the oven dish
2-3 teaspoons breadcrumbs

Wine: a full-bodied red wine, such as Campo de Borja from Alicante.

Place the stewing steak in a large pan with salted water, and add the bay leaf and peppercorns. Bring to the boil and gently simmer until tender. Then remove from the heat and allow to cool. Drain the meat and reserve the meat stock. Wash the peppers, discard the seeds and stalks and dry with kitchen paper. Chop the cooked meat very finely. Peel the onions and garlic, wash the parsley and chop them all finely. Dice the slices of bread, douse them with a few spoonfuls of stock and mash with a fork. Heat the butter in a frying-pan and fry the onions until golden-brown. Add the mince and stir. Then add the chopped stewing steak, the garlic, parsley and bread. Season with the thyme, salt and pepper and stir well together. Preheat the oven to 230°C/450°F/Gas Mark 8. When the mixture is cooked, fill the peppers with equal amounts of it and place them in a greased oven dish. Pour some of the stock over the dish and sprinkle with breadcrumbs. Bake in the oven for 25 minutes.

MAGRAS CON TOMATE

Sliced Ham in Tomato Sauce

In Spanish, *magro* means thin or slender. Thin slices of raw ham are used in this recipe.

200 g/7 oz raw sliced ham	Pepper
1 large onion	2 teaspoonfuls sugar
4 garlic cloves	2 hard-boiled eggs
200 g/7 oz tomatoes	
100 ml/3½ fl oz oil	**Wine:** a young red wine
30 g/1 oz pork dripping	perhaps from Ampurdán,
or lard	La Mancha
Salt	

Lay the slices of ham in a shallow flameproof casserole dish. Peel and finely chop the onions and garlic. Soak the tomatoes in boiling water for a few minutes. Skin and halve them, then seed them. Chop the tomato flesh into small pieces. Heat the oil and lard in a frying-pan and fry the onions, garlic and tomatoes . Sprinkle with the sugar, salt and pepper, stirring occasionally. Cook for 10 minutes. Pour this sauce into the casserole dish containing the ham. Gently cook over a low heat for another 15 minutes. Should the sauce become too dry, add a little water or red wine. Garnish with 2 chopped hard-boiled.

POLLO AL CHILINDRÓN

Chicken Stew with Paprika

Although *Pollo al chilindrón* is considered to be the classic Aragonian dish *par excellence* , it is relatively recent in origin, dating back to the days of the Spanish conquistadors, who brought the peppers and tomatoes which are so basic to this dish back to the Old World. *Chilindrón* was a card game that was very popular in the 17th century, and was played enthusiastically at picnics and festivals. The name *pollo al chilindrón* has been explained by the Aragonian cook Luis Bandrés, who claims that this dish was eaten whilst playing the card game of the same name. However the dish is no longer connected with the card game, although the recipe has remained almost exactly the same. It is usually made with chicken, but is occasionally made with lamb.

Serves 6	300 g/10 oz thin slices raw
	ham, finely chopped
3 oven-ready chickens	1 onion
200 ml/7 fl oz oil	6 sweet red peppers
1 clove garlic	
Salt	**Wine:** a robust red wine
Pepper	such as a Cariñena from
	Borja

Wash the chickens, dry them with kitchen paper and cut them into pieces. Heat the oil in a large casserole dish. Season the chicken pieces with salt and pepper and fry them all over until golden-brown. Peel the garlic, slice it and fry for a minute or two. Then add the chopped ham and the onion and continue to cook. Meanwhile, wash the peppers, seed them and slice them into thin strips. Add to the casserole and cover the pot. Stew, until the chicken is tender and the juice has evaporated, about 30 minutes.

CODORNIZ CON PIMIENTOS

Quail-stuffed Peppers

This dish used to be eaten mainly in late summer, the quail-hunting season when the birds are getting ready to migrate.

8 oven-ready quails	Salt
2 thick slices pork belly or	Pepper
raw ham	
200 ml/7 fl oz oil	**Wine:** a young quality
2 tablespoons cognac	red wine such as
8 large sweet red peppers	Valdepeñas from Navarra
6 tablespoons vegetable stock	

Preheat the oven to 200°C/400°F/Gas Mark 6. Wash the gutted quails. Dice the bacon or ham and stuff the quails with it. Heat the oil in a large pan and brown the quails on all sides on a low heat for 5 minutes. Then quickly flambé the birds on a high heat . Drain the oil used for frying the birds and reserve it. Meanwhile cut the stalk from the peppers, by cutting a cross in the base and remove the seeds. Place a quail inside each pepper and lay the quail-stuffed peppers in an ovenproof dish. Pour the reserved oil and the vegetable stock over the peppers and season with salt and pepper. Bake in the preheated oven for about 30 minutes and serve immediately.

CATALONIA

Catalonia is a region of great climatic contrast. In the Pyrenees, the climate is harsh, whereas in the delta of the River Ebro, temperatures are sub-tropical. This province in the north-eastern corner of the Iberian peninsula is distinguished from the other Spanish provinces by its extraordinarily varied cuisine in which both meat and fish dishes play a integral part. Soups are famous in this region, for example escudella i card d'olla, a filling soup containing unusual ingredients. There are also soups made with partridge, rabbit and various fish such as dried cod and monkfish. Often they are seasoned with thyme or mint. All these soups play an important role in Catalan cuisine. Other traditional dishes include duck with apples or dates and goose with pears. Lamb dishes are very popular, particularly those from the Gerona region, where lambs' feet are added to make an especially delicious dish.

Pork is another staple in the Catalan kitchen. It is used for its lard and also as the main ingredient in various well-known Catalan dishes such as lomo frito con alubias blancas, fried loin of pork with broad beans and the Pyrenean trixat amb rosta, cabbage with potatoes and bacon. Pork sausages also play an important part in Catalan cooking. The salami-type dry sausages known as salchichones de Vic are very popular, as are the similar fuet sausages. There is also butifarra blanca y negra, a black-and-white sausage which includes pigs' blood, bisbe, a sausage made of offal, tongue and fat, and butifarra catalan, a magnificent delicacy which includes truffles. At the other end of the gourmet spectrum,. the Catalans share a passion with the British for bacon and eggs.

Game is abundant and dishes made with it include perdiz con coles, partridge with cabbage roulade, conejo con peras, tender young rabbit with pears, liebre con castañas, hare with chestnuts and cordornices, quail prepared in a variety of ways.

Below: Even today bottled wines stored in the Cavas are turned by hand during the ageing period.

The coastal waters of Gerona are known for their abundance of different fish. However, for hundreds of years fish played a secondary role in Catalonia to pork, lamb, poultry and vegetables. For some time now fish dishes have become playing a greater part in the diet. There are salmonetes, (red mullet), sardinas, (sardines), caballas (mackerel) and anchoas, (anchovies). The best is probably mero (grouper) , which is prepared in a variety of ways. It can be grilled over charcoal, baked in the oven, shallow-fried or used as an ingredient in the unforgettable dish known as suquet. Suquet is a delicious fish broth, invented by the fishermen of Costa Brava, which can also be prepared with halibut, dogfish, and sea bream. A typical feature of Catalan cooking is the combination of meat and fish in a single dish, such as pollo y langosta, (chicken with crayfish). And of course there are many rice and seafood dishes.

The vegetable kingdom of Catalonia provides a firm foundation for tasty salads. These include espinacas a la catalana *(spinach with pine kernels and raisins)* and esclivada, *a cold vegetable platter, whose ingredients are grilled over charcoal, then peeled.* Sanfaina *sauce is a special delicacy, made with aubergines, courgettes, peppers, tomatoes and onions, which is a favourite when combined with chicken as* pollo con sanfaina.

Catalan desserts and sweets are very popular. There are exquisite, dark-chocolate Easter eggs called monas de Pascua *and the wonderful* panallets, *little cakes made with almonds, pine kernels and chocolate chips, amongst other things, which is eaten on All Saints' Day.* Turrón, *a cross between nougat and marzipan, is a typical Christmas sweet, which always includes almonds and sugar, but for which there are numerous recipes. On the saint's days of St John and St Peter,* tortells, *are baked in ring moulds.* Crema catalana *is a delicious version of burnt cream, a rich custard pudding with a caramelised topping, which was originally eaten on St Joseph's' day.*

Page 66/67: The Castillo de Tamarit in Tarragona.

Left: The museum in Sant Sadurní d'Anoia displays wine-making equipment dating from the beginning of the century.

Mediterranean Fish and Pork

Catalonia's landscape is varied, producing a range of climates from the alpine regions of the Pyrenees to the sub-tropical temperatures of Ebro delta. This is why Catalan cuisine is so varied, ranging from the seafood of the Mediterranean seaboard to the meat and game dishes of the interior.

Alongside *escudella i carn d'olla*, a hearty stew, there are soups flavoured with herbs, particularly with thyme. They are often made with partridge or rabbit, and there is also a dried cod and noodle soup and an excellent fish stew which contains. the delicious fish caught off Catalonia's rocky coastline. The most prized of these fish is monkfish, a popular delicacy in Barcelona.

There are also many poultry dishes such as duck stuffed with apple and goose cooked with pears.

Beef and ox meat from Gerona (famous, of course, for its bulls) tastes wonderful in the ragouts which also include lamb and calves' feet. The meat of the bulls is dark and strong, almost like venison.

Pork is an important ingredient in Catalonian cuisine and appears in many forms, including fried loin of pork with beans and bacon and eggs. In the Pyrenees, it is the main ingredient in *trinxat amb rosta*. Pork fat and lard are used in many dishes.

Pork sausages and delicatessen are a very important part of Catalan cuisine. The best-known sausage is a salami-type sausage from Vic called *fuet*. There is also the black-and-white *bisbe* sausage, a blood pudding. The most expensive is undoubtedly *butifarra*, a blood sausage seasoned with truffles which is used in many dishes.

The Mediterranean offers an almost unlimited variety of seafood. One of the most important fish from the coast of Gerona is sea bass, which can be baked, grilled, fried or cooked in fish stews such as *suquet*, in which grouper and bass are often included. There are also less expensive fish such as sardines, mackerel and anchovies.

Rice dishes are prepared in excitingly different ways. Delicious accompaniments include spider crab with fresh peas and a classic Catalan dish which includes crayfish and chicken.

The market gardens of Catalonia provide all the finest ingredients for salads and for the delicious spinach dish with pine kernels and raisins, which betrays a Moorish influence. Many salads include curly endive. One of the most popular Catalan dishes is chicken with *sanfaina.*, a vegetable mixture containing aubergines, courgettes and peppers.

In Catalonia cakes take precedence over desserts. There are towering Easter cakes and *panellets*, little marzipan cakes made only for All Saints' Day. The abundant almond orchards of Valencia and Catalonia provide the basic ingredient for *turrones*, dainty egg-shaped sweets, made with honey and almonds. There are the filled ring-shaped cakes baked for the feast days of San Juan and San Pedro and most prized of all the *crema catalana*, a burnt cream traditionally prepared for the feast of San José, but now available on the menu any day of the year. *Crema catalana* is popular all over Spain and even across the border in neighbouring France.

Pages 70/71: Typical
Catalonian fishing boats in
Cambril harbour.

Below right: The fresh catch
on display for sale in the
harbour.

SUQUET DE PEIX

Catalonian Fish Stew

Suquet de peix or *peix amb suc* literally translated means "fish in its own juice". This is a typical fisherman's dish from the Costa Brava and its preparation requires a lot of time and skill on the part of the cooks and housewives of the region. It is one of those hearty fish dishes typical of Mediterranean cuisine

Approx 750 g/1½ lb monkfish, red mullet or rascasse, scaled and gutted, with heads
1 medium-sized fennel bulb

Salt	60 g/2 oz shelled, blanched
250 g/½ lb potatoes	almonds
2 onions	45 g/1½ oz monkfish liver
6 garlic cloves	12 mussels
1 hot red chilli pepper	6 cooked scampi (giant
1 slice white bread, crusts	prawns)
removed	
1-2 tablespoons olive oil	**Wine:** a full-bodied white
Oil for frying	such as a Rueda from La
	Mancha

Cut the heads off the fish and reserve them. Wash and quarter the fennel. Bring 2 litres/3½ pints of water to the boil in a large saucepan and add the fennel and fish heads. Season lightly with salt, cover the pan and simmer for about 30 minutes, skimming the foam that rises to the surface from time to time. Then cut the fish into 6 slices and season with salt. Peel, wash and slice the potatoes. Peel the onions and cut them into rings. Peel 3 of the garlic cloves. Trim and seed the chilli pepper and chop it finely. Arrange the potato slices, onion rings, garlic, chilli and fish slices in a flameproof casserole dish Strain the fish stock through a fine sieve into the casserole until the liquid comes half-way up the sides of the pot. Add the oil, cover the pot, and cook on a high heat for 20 minutes. Meanwhile, heat the oil for frying and fry the white bread on both sides until crisp. Remove the bread and replace it with the monkfish liver. Fry for 2 or 3 minutes. Chop the remaining 3 cloves of garlic, dice the fried bread, mash the liver and mix well with the almonds. Add this mixture, along with the mussels and the whole scampi, to the casserole. As soon as the mussels open, the stew is ready to serve.

SOPA DE RAPE

Monkfish Soup

1 onion	250g/8 oz watercress,
2 medium-sized tomatoes	1-2 slices day-old bread,
1.6 kg/3½ lb fish heads	crusts removed
(monkfish or hake if possible)	30g/1 oz blanched almonds
2 tablespoons oil	1 bunch parsley

3 garlic cloves
1 small piece monkfish liver
Oil

Wine: a full-bodied white wine such as Rioja de Crianza from Alella

Peel and finely chop the onions. Chop the tomatoes into small pieces. Wash and dry the watercress and chop it coarsely Bring 3 litres/5½ pints of water to the boil, wash the fish heads and throw them in the pot. Heat the oil in a frying-pan and brown the onions; add the watercress and tomatoes. Add the mixture to the fish stock, season with salt and cook on low heat for 15-20 minutes, uncovered, skimming off the foam from time to time. Meanwhile, crumble the dried bread into breadcrumbs. Strain the fish stock through a fine sieve into another pot and thicken it with the breadcrumbs. Remove the flesh from the fish heads, divide it up between 4 soup bowls and keep them warm. Wash the parsley and shake it dry. Peel the garlic. Fry the fish liver in a little oil for 2 minutes, then chop it finely along with the parsley and garlic and add to the broth. Cook for another 15 minutes then pour the stock over the fish in the soup bowls and serve immediately.

PERDIZ CON COLES

Partridge with Stuffed Cabbage

2 oven-ready partridges	125 ml/4 fl oz meat or
Salt	vegetable stock
Pepper	1 green cabbage
100 ml/3½ fl oz olive oil	1 egg, beaten with 1
100 g/3½ oz pork dripping	teaspoon water
or lard	60 g/2 oz flour
150 g/5 oz bacon, diced	oil for frying
1 large onion	
2 medium-sized carrots	**Wine:** a fine vintage wine
1 bouquet garni	(*de reserva*) such as
60 ml/2 fl oz brandy	Méntrida from Borja

Wipe the partridges inside and out with a damp cloth and season with salt and pepper. Heat the olive oil and lard in a flameproof casserole and fry the partridges and diced bacon until golden-brown. Peel and chop the onion. Wash and peel the carrots and cut them into thick slices. Add them, along with the bouquet garni, to the pot and fry until golden-brown. Then add the brandy, cook for two minutes then add the stock. Cover and continue to cook on a low heat for at least another hour. Meanwhile, cut out the stem of the cabbage and remove the leaves, discarding the outermost ones. Wash the leaves and blanch them in salted water for about 10 minutes until they are tender. Drain and leave them to dry. Roll the cabbage leaves up tightly, pressing them together firmly into round parcels or roulades. First dip the cabbage rolls in the beaten egg, then in the flour. Fry the rolls in hot oil. Remove the partridges from the pot and arrange them in a large warmed serving dish. Garnish with the rolled cabbage leaves and carrot slices. Strain the cooking liquid from the pot through a sieve over the partridges and serve piping hot.

CONEJO CON PERAS

Rabbit with Pears

If fresh rabbit is not available, you can use frozen rabbit portions.

1 oven-ready rabbit	
Salt	1 garlic clove
Pepper	1 bunch parsley, chopped
125 ml/4 fl oz oil	15 g/1 oz almonds,
250g/8 oz carrots	chopped
250g/8 oz onions	15 g/ 1 oz hazelnuts,
60 g/2 oz leeks	chopped
30 g/1 oz celery	
6 pears (approx 650/11/2 lb)	**Wine:** a mature good
60 ml/2 fl oz dry white wine	quality wine (*de reserva*)
900 ml/11/2 pints meat stock	such as Priorato from Yecla

Slice the rabbit into 6- 8 pieces. Sprinkle the pieces with salt and pepper. Heat the oil in a flameproof casserole and fry the pieces until golden-brown. Remove the pan from the heat remove the rabbit pieces and reserve them in a bowl. Cover them and put them in a warm place. Wash and clean the vegetables and chop them into small pieces. Wash and core 2 of the pears and cut them into small pieces. Fry them along with the vegetables. Add the wine and stock, the peeled garlic, the parsley and chopped nuts and leave to cook for another 15 minutes. Return the rabbit pieces to the casserole and strain the sauce over them. Season again to taste. Place the casserole on a medium heat and cook for another 15-20 minutes, turning the rabbit from time to time. Meanwhile slice the remaining pears in half and core them. Add them to the pot 3 minutes before the end of the cooking time.

POLLO CON SANFAINA

Chicken with Mixed Vegetables

Catalonian *sanfaina* is not to be confused with the Castilian dish made with egg yolks.

1 large chicken, approx
1.2 kg/2½ lb
Salt
Pepper
200 ml/7 fl oz oil
300 g/10 oz onions
1 garlic clove
1 bay leaf
400 g/14 oz ripe tomatoes
100 ml/3½ fl oz white wine
125 ml/4 fl oz stock
300 g/10 oz large red or
green sweet peppers
300 g/10 oz courgettes
300 g/10 oz aubergine
100 g/3½ oz flour

Wine: a Rosé or young red
wine such as Ribiero, La
Mancha

Wash the chicken, pat it dry with kitchen paper, divide into 8 serving pieces and season all over with salt and pepper. Heat about half the oil in a casserole and fry the chicken pieces until golden-brown. Peel the onions and cut them into thick slices. Peel and chop the garlic and add it with the onions and bay leaf to the chicken. Fry until the onion is golden-brown. Place the tomatoes in boiling water, skin them and chop them finely. Stir the tomatoes into the chicken mixture and cook for a short while. Add the wine, stir and bring to the boil, then add the stock. Reduce the heat and leave to simmer. In the meantime, brush the peppers with oil and grill them on a high heat until the skin is blackened and will easily separate from the flesh. Peel the courgettes and the aubergine, skin the peppers and finely dice them all. Season the vegetables with salt, dip them in flour and fry in a frying-pan in the rest of the oil until golden-brown. Add the vegetables to the casserole and continue to simmer until the chicken is cooked, about 30 minutes.

ARROZ A LA CASSOLA

Catalonian Risotto

2 tablespoons oil
200 g/7 oz pork chops
200 g/7 oz rabbit pieces
4 medium-sized or 8 small

prawns
1 medium-sized squid
1 medium-sized onion
2 ripe tomatoes
1 garlic clove
1 tablespoon chopped parsley

400 g/14 oz short-grained rice
150 g/5 oz clams
300 g/10 oz peas (fresh or frozen)

Wine: a young red wine such as a Ribera del Duero from Tarragona

Heat the oil in a casserole dish. Trim the excess fat from the pork chops, cut the rabbit into serving pieces and brown all the meat in the hot oil. Remove meat from pan. Wash the prawns. Clean the squid, discard the "beak" and cut it into small pieces. Fry the seafood in the oil then remove and reserve it. Peel and chop the onions. Dip the tomatoes in boiling water, skin and chop them. Peel the garlic and chop it. Then chop the parsley. Fry the onions in the oil until golden-brown and add the garlic, tomatoes and parsley in succession. Add the rice, stir and cook for 10 minutes.

Meanwhile wash the mussels and scrape off the beards. Steam the mussels in a little water until they open, discarding any which remain shut. Cook the peas for 5 minutes in 1½ litres/2½ pints of salted, boiling water. Add the clams and the peas with their cooking water to the casserole containing the rice. Return the browned meat and add the cooked shellfish to the pot and cook on a high heat for 15 minutes. Remove the risotto from the heat and let it stand for 3 minutes before serving.

FIDEUS A LA CASSOLA

Catalonian Noodle Hotpot

300 g/10 oz pork chops, trimmed of excess fat
1 tablespoon oil
125 ml/4 fl oz veal or vegetable stock
150 g/5 oz sausage meat
3 ripe tomatoes

480 g/1 lb tagliatelle
Salt
Pepper

Wine: a full-bodied, dry white wine from Albarino or a young red wine from Valdepeñas

Chop the pork chops into small pieces and brown all over in the oil in a casserole. Peel and chop the onions and brown them with the pork. Add the stock, bring to the boil and simmer until the pork is tender, adding a little more water if neccessary. Add the sausage meat and cook for a few minutes more. Soak the tomatoes in boiling water, skin and finely chop. Add them to the pot and cook for a further ten minutes. Then stir in the noodles and

cook for a few minutes more. Pour in enough water to cover the ingredients and cook on a high heat until the noodles are *al dente*. Season with salt and pepper.

ENSALADAS DE LENTEJAS

Lentil Salad

Despite the name this is more of a stew than a salad. The ham can be omitted, making it a vegetarian dish.

300 g/10 oz lentils
1 large onion
2 cloves
1 bay leaf
1 small sprig thyme
3 carrots
3 turnips
1 stick celery
Salt
5 black peppercorns

2 thick leeks
1 slice raw ham
1 shallot
1 bunch chives
1 tablespoon vinegar
½ teaspoon mustard
2-3 tablespoons olive oil

Wine: a fruity white wine such as a Rueda from Alella

Soak the lentils for several hours or overnight, then rinse them in fresh water. Peel and dice the onion. S crape and dice 1 carrot and 1 turnip. Put the vegetables in a large pot with the washed celery, lentils, cloves, bay leaf, thyme, ½ teaspoon salt, the peppercorns and enough water to cover the ingredients. Boil the lentils and vegetables until tender, then drain them. Wash, scrape and finely dice the remaining carrots and turnips, then finely chop the leeks. Cooked the chopped vegetables on a gentle in a little salted boiling water. Dice the ham and add it to the lentils with the cooked vegetables. Peel and finely chop the shallot. Chop the chives and add them with the shallot, the vinegar, a few pinches of salt, the mustard and the oil to the lentils. Stir the ingredients thoroughly to combine and the lentil salad is ready to serve.

ESPINACAS A LA CATALANA

Catalonian Spinach

Spinach is a popular winter vegetable in hot countries. The Catalonians have an interesting recipe for this otherwise simple winter vegetable, made with raisins from Malaga, pine nuts and black pepper.

1.4 kg/3 lb spinach
150 ml/5 fl oz olive oil
1 garlic clove
100g/3½ oz pine nuts

100g/3½ oz raisins
Salt
Black pepper

Cook the well-washed spinach in salted water for 7-8 minutes. Drain it in a colander and chop it finely. Heat the olive oil in a frying-pan and fry the peeled garlic until golden brown and then remove it and discard it. Add the pine nuts and raisins to the oil and fry until the raisins swell. Then add the spinach and continue to cook on a low heat, stirring occasionally, until the spinach it is heated through. Season with salt and pepper before serving.

BUÑUELOS DEL AMPURDÁN

Ampurdán Doughnuts

15g/½ oz fresh yeast or
1 sachet dried yeast
100 ml/3½ fl oz milk
360 g/12 oz flour, sifted
3 eggs
60 g/2 oz sugar
60 g/2 oz softened butter
1 lemon rind grated

1 teaspoon brandy
Approx 500 ml/16 fl oz oil for frying
Icing sugar

Wine: a fine dessert wine or a sparkling white wine such as Jumilla from Cariñena

All the ingredients for the dough must be at room temperature before starting. In a large bowl combine the yeast with the milk, stir in 150 g/5 oz of the sifted flour, cover with a damp cloth and leave for 20 minutes. Gradually mix this leaven with the rest of the flour, the eggs, sugar, butter, grated lemon peel and brandy and knead the mixture into a dough. Knead the dough until it is elastic and no longer sticks to your fingers. Leave the dough to stand in a warm place, covered with a damp cloth for 3 hours or until doubled in bulk. Knock back the dough and shape it into lumps the shape and size of ping-pong balls. On floured surface, roll these into finger-thick sausages and join the ends to make doughnut rings on a floured surface. Leave the rings to prove for about 30 minutes .

To cook the doughnuts, heat the oil in a deep-fryer and when it reaches the right temperature (a one-inch cube of bread should brown in 60 seconds) fry the rings on both sides. Remove them when golden-brown, and them on kitchen paper . Sprinkle generously with icing sugar and serve as quickly as possible.

CREMA CATALANA

Catalonian Burnt Cream

Crema catalana is Catalonia's best known dessert. This egg custard is allegedly of Spanish-Jewish origin. It used to be made only on festival days as a special dessert, particularly on St Joseph's day (19th March). Today it is eaten everywhere and on all occasions. Some Catalonian gourmets prefer to leave the crispy caramel topping off the custard, considering that it makes the pudding too sweet,. Others maintain that the topping is what makes the dish so special.

Serves 8

1 litre/1 pint 15 fl oz milk
8 egg yolks
1 teaspoon vanilla essence
1 teaspoon almond essence
½ grated lemon rind

250g/8 oz castor sugar
1 tablespoon ground cinnamon

Wine: a fine dessert wine or a *Cava,* a Champagne-style sparkling white wine

Whisk the egg yolks with the milk, vanilla and almond essences, grated lemon peel and sugar until foaming. Slowly heat the mixture in a saucepan, stirring continuously, until it begins to thicken. Remove it from the heat. Fill ovenproof ramekin dishes with the mixture. For the caramelised version, sprinkle with a thin layer of sugar and dust with cinnamon. Place the bowls under a preheated grill and cook until the sugar caramelises and bubbles. Serve warm.

CASTILE AND LEÓN

*O*ld Castile and León have a solid, established cuisine. The region is known as el gran zona de los asados, *the main region for roast meat dishes, particularly lamb and pork. There is a partiality for the meat of young animals. The sheep are barely one year old, sometimes only weeks old and suckling pigs only a few weeks old are adeptly oven-roasted. Not only roasts make an appearance on the table here, so do lamb dishes such as caldereta de cordero a la pastora, which is usually prepared in an earthenware casserole dish. There are various special pork dishes, ranging from the* chorizo *sausage from Cantimpalos,* serrano *ham, suckling pig from Guijelo,* morcillas *from Burgos, to the unmistakable Segovian bean stew* judiones de la Granja.

*T*he extensive culinary offerings of Castile and the kingdom of Léon include an exquisite variety of fowl and freshwater fish. The pigeons from the region of Palencia and Valladolid are very popular as are the trout from the rivers Tiétar and Tormes, and especially the trout from the Pueblo de Sanabria. Delicious tench thrive in the deep waters of clear

Page 78/79: The magnificent Alcázar in Segovia.

Right: A stone oven in which bread is baked and meat is roasted, using wood as fuel, giving them a delicious smoky flavour.

Below: A dovecote in the high plains of Meseta.

lagoons. The pececillos, *small fish from the river Adaja are well known, as is the taste of the freshwater crabs from Burgos.*

*C*astile-Léon is also famed for its tortillas, *the typical Spanish omelettes and for its* huevos revueltos con esparragos trigueros, *poached eggs with green asparagus.* Migas canas *is an ancient dish consisting of cubes of bread cubes soaked in milk and fried which was invented by shepherds. Although sweet dishes are not as popular in Old Castile as in some other parts of Spain, the nuns have created some delicious desserts, such as the exquisite custards and the* yemas de Avila, de Almanzán *and* de Segovia *which are made of sugar and egg yolks.*

Left :The Plaza Mayor in Salamanca is the most beautiful in Spain.

81

Lamb and Suckling Pig

As you explore the various regions of Spain and get to know the most important Spanish dishes of the Peninsula, you will discover that the quality of the local meat has not always been of the best An improvement in the quality of lamb was made possible by better transport links and the strong almost unbearable aftertaste of old, tough mutton that was not fresh has been eradicated. Nowadays, one can order lamb in most Spanish restaurants without a second thought. Lamb cutlets and leg of lamb or the various grilled lamb dishes all taste as good as they look. In Old Castile lamb has always been so outstandingly succulent that it has almost become a cult in the Castilian kitchen.

The sucking-pig and pork from this region has always been excellent. An indication of its popularity is the various names for it, as many as seven - *cerdo, tostón, cochinillo, puerco, marrano, guarro* and *lechón*. Old Castile was famous for its pigs as long ago as Roman times. The famous Roman gourmet, Apicius, mentions sucking-pig in his recipe collection and it has graced the tables of kings and cardinals, although today it can be enjoyed by everyone. The famous master chef, Cándido, now well into his eighties, guides people through the great art of cooking sucking-pig in his *Méson* in the shadow of the grand aquaduct of Segovia. He explains how the fuel used to heat the oven should be either pine wood, thyme branches or gorse, and quotes the proverb, *"El lechón, del cuchillo al asador"* which means "the shorter the interval between the slaughter and the cooking of the sucking-pig the better the flavour". The roasted animal with its caramel-coloured skin is brought to the table whole, where the master Cándido with a triumphant expression carves into the animal using the edge of a plate. There is no better way of demonstrating the quality or the tenderness of the meat, which must be removed from the oven at exactly the right moment.

Right: Herds of sheep dominate the landscape of the barren plains of Castile.

Below (1): Sheep grazing as they would have done in the days of old around the Castillo de Coca.

Below (2): Young suckling lambs with the ewe.

When it comes to the preparation of lamb dishes, the Castilians value the traditional recipes, which are sublimely different. A particularly tasty speciality is *pierna de cordero rellena*, stuffed leg of lamb, filled with spinach, tomatoes, eggs and raw ham, flavoured with garlic and a glass of sherry. Castile and Léon have essentially remained farming areas. The every day mentality of the villages of Old Castile is still light years away from the culinary metropolis of Madrid. Without a doubt, despite technical advances, the farmers are still down to earth, in tune with the seasons and dependant on the natural world.

The cuisine of Old Castile and Léon relies on simple preparation methods for delicious raw ingredients. Complex, ingenious "creations" have no place on these stony, high plateaux where priority is given to animal husbandry and hunting. The rugged nature of the traditional roasts and stews suits the broad landscape perfectly. Those who love life away from the hustle and bustle of the city and are stout-hearted, able to withstand the bitterly cold winters and scorching hot summers, will appreciate the flavours of these simple dishes.

A good example of the food of Old Castile and León is *sofrit payés*, a typical farmers' stew containing lamb, chicken, sausages and potatoes, flavoured with a few herbs and spices. As a general rule, the meat is stewed for several hours in a cast iron pot before being is served. The result is hearty, homely Castilian fare.

Spain is not generally noted for its potato dishes. Of course, with the advent of tourism and seaside resorts, the chip has become popular in the most frequent tourist haunts, although fortunately it has not managed to displace the traditional *tortilla* in rural areas.

Castile is the bastion of the Spanish tortilla. If one encounters a *tortilla española* on the menu, it will be a Castilian recipe. Parallels can be drawn between the tortilla and the pizza, whose Neapolitan origins have been equally forgotten in the midst of its world-wide popularity. Furthermore, both dishes were introduced to Europe by the Arabs. The roots of the tortilla take us back to the Old Castilian kitchen; thinly sliced potatoes splutter in oil, finely chopped onions are added and the beaten eggs are stirred in under the potato layers, whilst seasonings are added for extra flavour. Then with a deft flip, the lightly-browned tortilla is lifted in the air and on to a plate, then allowed to slide back into the pan upside down so that the other side may lightly brown in the olive oil.

The Spanish tortilla is served as a complete meal in itself, and there are no limits to what may be added. Tortillas may be filled with ingredients as varied as mushrooms and asparagus, sausage and ham, or with crab. That is yet another way in which the tortilla is the Spanish equivalent of the pizza.

CALDERETA DE CORDERO A LA PASTORA

Shepherds' Lamb Stew

This is a traditional shepherds' stew, usually prepared out in the fields beneath the huge canopy of the sky. The ingredients used in this dish are garlic, thyme and shoulder of lamb, lambs' liver and brains. It is a hearty, warming dish for the cold winter months, well-seasoned with black pepper and Cayenne.

Serves 6

250 ml/8 fl oz suckling lamb
1 onion
2 kg/4½ lb shoulder of lamb
120 g/4 oz lambs' liver
2 tablespoons breadcrumbs
1 tablespoon
 Cayenne pepper
2 tablespoons vinegar
4 garlic cloves

½ lamb's brain

1 teaspoon dried thyme or few sprigs fresh thyme
Salt
Freshly-ground black pepper

Wine: a full-bodied red wine such as Almansa or Borja

Heat the oil in a large, flameproof casserole. Cut the lamb shoulder into 60 g/2 oz cubes, chop the liver very finely and add them both to the oil. Fry for 10 minutes. Add the breadcrumbs, paprika and vinegar. Peel and chop the garlic finely. Chop the brains. Stir in the garlic, brains and thyme to the casserole and add enough water to cover the ingredients. Season with salt and pepper and simmer for 40 minutes. Then remove the stew from the heat, cover and leave to stand for another hour. Reheat before serving.

LECHAZO CASTELLANO

Castilian Milk-fed Lamb

½ young lamb
(approx 1.5 kg/3 lb)
1 tablespoon pork dripping or lard
Salt

Wine: full-bodied, if possible a good quality vintage red wine such as a Ribera del Duero from Rioja

Place the lamb, skin side down, in a large stewpan with a tight-fitting and add 250 ml/8 fl oz water, salt and the fat. Cover the pan with aluminium foil and then add the lid, so the pot is seal. Cook on a very low heat for 1½ hours. Remove the foil and lid, turn the lamb over and salt the outside of the meat. Cook for another 20 minutes, uncovered, on high heat, turning so that the meat is evenly browned.

SOPA CASTELLANA

Castilian Soup

Serves 6

100 g/3½ oz pork dripping
 or lard or some oil
3 garlic cloves
100 g/3½ oz lean ham
6 small slices of day-
old bread

1 tablespoon paprika
1 litre/1¾ pints stock
6 eggs
Caraway seeds (optional)

Wine: a dry white wine or Rosé such as Ribiero from Albarino

Melt the lard in a large saucepan. Peel and slice the garlic and fry until golden brown. Dice the ham, add to the pot with the slices of bread and fry for a few minutes. Sprinkle with the paprika, add the stock and stir well. Season with salt and simmer for 10 minutes. Preheat the oven to a 200°C/400°F/Gas Mark 6. Pour the soup into 6 ovenproof soup bowls and carefully crack an egg on top of each soup. Put the bowls into the oven and leave for 3 minutes or until the egg white solidifies. Sprinkle with caraway if desired and serve piping hot.
The soup can be oven heated in one large pot, if liked.

PICHONES ASADOS

Baked Pigeons

250 g/8 oz lentils
4 young pigeons,
 with giblets
4 tablespoons pork
fat or lard
8 garlic cloves
1 bay leaf
½ teaspoon oregano
1 tablespoon brandy

4 tablespoons stock
Salt
Pepper

Wine: a good quality vintage red wine (*de reserva*) such as Penedès from Rioja

Soak the lentils for a few hours in cold water for at least 2 hours before cooking. Heat the fat in a casserole dish and add the garlic, oregano and bay leaf. Wash the pigeons and dry inside and out with kitchen paper. Add them to the casserole and fry them all over on a high heat until they are golden-brown. Reduce the heat to low add the offal and cook for a few minutes. Add the brandy and stock and stir. Cover the casserole and continue to cook on a low heat until the birds are done. Meanwhile, drain the lentils and put them in a pot with enough water to cover them. Cook them until they are soft, about 40 minutes. Drain them and season with salt and pepper. Serve the pigeons on a bed of lentils.

COCHINILLO ASADO

Sucking Pig

Serves 6

1 sucking pig
6 bay leaves
60 g/2 oz pork dripping
or lard
Salt

Pepper
2 garlic cloves

Wine: a good quality
vintage wine (*de reserva*)
such as Ribera del Duero
from Rioja

Preheat the oven to 190°C/375°F/Gas Mark 5. Pour 200 ml/7 fl oz water into a roasting pan and add the bay leaves. Brush the sucking pig inside and out with the softened lard and rub with salt and pepper. Put the meat and the unpeeled garlic cloves in the roasting pan and roast in the oven. The high fat content of the meat requires it to cook slowly, hence the fairly low oven temperature and the water, so that it can roast in its own juices. The meat is cooked when the juices have almost entirely dried up. To get a crispy crackling, stick a needle in the skin when the meat has reached the stage where it becomes golden brown. This will release any air which builds up in the fat underneath the skin.

TRUCHAS ESCABECHADAS

Marinated Trout

The recipe for this marinade (*Escabeche*) was probably brought to the Spanish mainland by the Moors. Marinades and spices were used to preserve fish and other foods. The basic recipe for *escabeche* is always the same - wine and vinegar, oil, herbs and spices.

Serves 6

6 trout, gutted and cleaned,
each weighing about
200 g/7 oz
Salt
Freshly-ground
black pepper
2 tablespoons flour,
sifted
300 ml/10 fl oz oil
for frying
4 garlic cloves

3 bay leaves
1 bunch parsley,
coarsely chopped
1 teaspoon dried thyme
or few sprigs fresh thyme
200 ml/7 fl oz fish stock
200 ml/7 fl oz white wine
200 ml/7 floz vinegar

Wine: To complement the
acidic marinade, beer is
recommended rather than
wine.

Wash the trout, dry it with kitchen paper and rub it with the salt and pepper. Lightly coat the fish in the sifted flour and fry them in one third of the oil. When cooked, reserve them in a large shallow dish in a warm place. Heat the remaining oil in another pan and brown the peeled garlic, the bay leaf, thyme and the parsley. Douse with the wine, vinegar and stock and cook, uncovered on fairly high heat, until the liquid has reduced by half. Pour the marinade over the fish. Leave to marinate for 24 hours in the refrigerator and serve very cold.

YEMAS DE SEGOVIA

Segovian Sweetmeats

Serves 8

200 g/7 oz castor sugar
Grated rind of
1 lemon or 1 orange
16 egg yolks
250 g/8 oz icing sugar

Chocolate shavings,
to decorate (optional)

Wine: a fine semisweet
dessert wine such as an
oloroso sherry

Put the castor sugar, 16 teaspoons of water (1 per egg yolk) and the grated rind in a small saucepan and boil until the syrup is thick. It should form a soft ball when a little is dropped into cold water.

Whisk the egg yolks in a bowl until foaming and strain them through a fine sieve into a bain-marie or the top of a double-boiler. Bring the water underneath bain-marie gently to the boil. Stir the syrup into the egg yolks and stir the mixture constantly as it gradually thickens. When it has a porridge-like consistency, remove the pan from the heat and leave to cool. Work the icing sugar into the cooled the mixture. With wetted hands, take walnut-sized pieces of the mixture and shape them into small round ballsor pyramids. Arrange these in confectionery paper cups. The *yemas* can be sprinkled with chocolate shavings, if liked.

HUEVOS CON ESPÁRRAGOS TRIGUEROS

Poached Eggs with Asparagus

Espárrago triguero is the Spanish name for the green asparagus or sprue, which grows wild in many parts of the Spanish mainland. It is often accompanied by a *tortilla* (Spanish omelette) or, as in this recipe, by poached eggs.

Serves 6

4 bunches asparagus
Salt
12 eggs
100 ml/3 fl oz vinegar
175 ml/6 fl oz oil
4 garlic cloves
½ tablespoon sweet paprika

1 tablespoon vinegar

Wine: wine is not usually drunk with asparagus but if you are going to do so anyway, then choose a young red wine or a Rosé, perhaps something from Ribera del Duero

Cook the asparagus in boiling salted water until firm but tender. At the same time, poach the eggs in a poacher. Alternatively, in shallow pan, bring 1 litre/1¾ pints of water, to the boil and add a level teaspoon of salt and the vinegar. Bring back to the boil. Crack each egg separately into a cup, and carefully slip them one by one into the boiling water; poach for 3 minutes. Meanwhile, peel and coarsely chop the garlic and fry it in the oil until golden brown . Stir the paprika into the oil and add a tablespoon of vinegar to make a sauce. When the eggs are ready, remove them with a slotted spoon. Place the eggs and drained asparagus in a large shallow heatproof dish and pour the sauce over them. Reheat briefly under a hot grill before serving.

JUDIONES DE LA GRANJA

Castilian Bean Stew

If fresh pigs' ears and trotters are not available, use pickled ones, but soak them in two changes of water for 24 hours and drain well before cooking.

Serves 6

480 g/1 lb dried
broad beans
1 pig's ear
1 pig's trotter
100g/3½ oz chorizo sausage
100g/3½ oz Serrano or
other raw ham
1 medium-sized tomato
200 ml/7 fl oz olive oil
1 onion

1 clove garlic
1 pickled pepper
1 bunch parsley
1 bay leaf
1 tablespoon mild
paprika
1 tablespoon flour

Wine: a full-bodied red wine such as Almansa from Alicante

Soak the broad beans in cold water overnight. Drain them

and discard the soaking water. Boil the beans in fresh water on a high heat for 30 minutes and drain thoroughly. Cut the pigs' ear and trotter, ham and chorizo sausage into small pieces. Add to a large pan, then add the beans and boiling water to cover. Cook until the meat and beans are tender, then drain. Skin the tomato in boiling water and chop finely. Chop the peeled onion and garlic. Finely chop the pepper and the parsley. Heat the oil in a pan and fry the vegetables, garlic, parsley, bay leaf, paprika and flour together, stirring the sauce until it is smooth and the vegetables are soft. Pour this sauce over the beans and pork, stir it in and season with salt. Simmer on a low heat for 30 minutes, adding a little water should the stew become too dry. Remove from the heat, cover and leave to stand for a further half hour before serving.

CANGREJOS DE RÍO AL ESTILO DE BURGOS

Burgos Freshwater Crabs

Freshwater crabs are scarce in Britain and are consequently very expensive. The seasonal time for them is in summer from 24 June onwards.

1 onion	Black pepper
360 g/12 oz tomatoes	Salt
100 ml/3½ fl oz oil	
24 freshwater crabs	**Wine:** a robust, dry white
60 ml/2 fl oz brandy	wine such as Alella from
1/2 pepper	La Mancha
12 whole cloves, pounded	
in a mortar	

Peel and chop the onion. Drop the tomatoes in boiling water and skin them. Push them through a sieve. Heat the oil in a large flameproof casserole and brown the onions. Add the crabs and douse with the brandy. Stir in the puréed tomatoes, the chopped pepper, the pounded cloves and ground pepper. Season with salt. Cook the crabs for 10 minutes. Serve hot in a deep dish.

VALENCIA, MURCIA

The Levante, which is in the centre of Spain's eastern coast, is the main rice-growing region of Spain. It is thus known in culinary terms as la zona de arroces, *the region of rice dishes. The world-famous rice dish* paella *naturally comes from these parts, or to be more accurate, it originates from the province of Valencia. However, there are many other rice dishes from the region which taste just as good. They include* arroz con costra *(Oven-baked rice)*, arroz con fesols i naps *(Rice with green beans and turnips) and* arroz a banda *(Rice in fish stock). The provinces of Valencia and Murcia have plenty of fish and shellfish to offer, including crayfish from the shores of Vinaroz in Castellón, which are amongst the best in the whole of Spain. There are also mussels and eels, which are prepared here with garlic and pepper. Snails and frogs' legs are also eaten. Of course, Valencia is also famous for its juicy oranges and there is a deliciously fruity, refreshing orange sorbet which comes from the province.*

Murcia has a region of market gardens called huertas, *which were originally developed by the Moors. The local dish here is* tortilla a la murciana, *a vegetable omelette. There are also plenty of delicious colourful salads and the garlic grown here is of particularly fine quality. A sensational garlic sauce incorporating olive oil and breadcrumbs is made from the local garlic. The local sheep and lamb which graze in the pastures of the region are also made into delicious dishes as are chicken and rabbit. The region makes sausage specialities not to be found elsewhere in Spain, such as the dish cooked* obispo (bishop-style), in which sausage is stuffed into a pork stomach. The *Mar Menor* off Murcia produces wonderful seafood. Along this coast, smoked roe is a favourite delicacy and one can sometimes even get treats such as Iranian caviar.

Overleaf: Landscape
in Totona (Murcia).

Right: The rocky retreat
of Guadalest near
Alicante.

Below: Orange groves
dominate the landscape
in the Levante.

Rice and Saffron

Rice has been the main staple grain used in oriental cuisine for centuries. It has been cultivated in China since before 2500 BC and slowly made its way across to Europe over the centuries. It was introduced to Spain by the Arabs. The Moors started cultivating it here, along with herbs and saffron, the precious, costly reddish-yellow herb that was so important in the rest of Europe in the Middle Ages. The Moors also passed on to the Spanish their love of preparing sweet-and-sour combinations in food.

Saffron, a member of the crocus family, was originally found only in the wild, but it has been cultivated for centuries and has been used in the kitchen to add colour and aroma. The ancient Greeks and Romans praised it highly. Spain has been cultivating saffron longer than any other country in Europe.

Italian recipes for rice dishes are more elaborate than their Spanish counterparts, and Valencia is at the forefront of Spanish rice cuisine. It is an established historical fact that Valencian farmers introduced rice to Catalonia. The crowning glory of Valencian rice dishes has to be *paella* with its opulent variety of ingredients and only a Valencian or someone who has been taught by one knows how to achieve the right balance in cooking this dish. When the Arab invaders discovered that there were raisins and dates in Spain, that the Mediterranean yielded fish, mussels and crabs and that there were rabbits and chickens in abundance, they experimented with all the ingredients at once. This eventually produced a dish called *paella*. Its creation reflects the multicultural nature of Spanish life, which these days is based on tolerance and peaceful coexistence.

The common link between *Paella valenciana* and the Italian *Risotto alla milanese* is the use of saffron. It was either the Phoenicians or the Arabs who first introduced saffron to Spain. The word saffron is of Arabic origin and is known by this name all over western Europe, whilst the Latin name "crocus" has virtually been forgotten.

Saffron lends colour and charm to a variety of rice dishes, but above all to the *paella*. Nowadays, saffron is the most expensive spice in the world and it is used as a propitious, subtly-flavoured colouring agent.

Bullfights, Flamenco, football, sherry and paella represent Spanish life in a nutshell for many tourists. Those people who see Spain in this light have merely scratched the surface.

Nevertheless if you want to taste Spain's very soul, eating *paella* is an excellent way of doing so. The best *paellas* are cooked in Valencia- at least, so the Valencians say . And who is going to argue with them? Perhaps a Catalonian or an Andalusian!

Facing page: Rice cultivation is always hard work in the Ebro Delta.

Left: After the harvest the rice is laid out to dry.

Below: Strands of saffron.

PAELLA VALENCIANA

Valencian Paella

Paella valenciana is the most famous of all Spanish dishes There are many ways to prepare this hearty, appetising main course. Traditionally, it is cooked outdoors, on an open fire. Its preparation requires balance and good judgement as to quantities and cooking times. The experts know that if the dish is to be "right ", the rice should still be "al dente" despite the fact that it takes a shorter time to cook than the other ingredients. It takes practice to capture that authentic Spanish flavour.

200 ml/7 fl oz oil
Salt
1 chicken, cut into 8 pieces
150 g/ 5 oz smoked pork loin, chopped
4 chipolata sausages
4 cubes of ham
1 red or green pepper
1 garlic clove
150g/5 oz French beans
2 artichokes, trimmed
120 g/4 oz squid, cleaned , boned and thinly sliced
3 medium-sized tomatoes
1 tablespoon paprika
2 dozen snails.
4 shrimps
18 clams
12 mussels
400 g/14 oz round-grained rice
100g/3½ fresh or frozen peas
4 small pieces monkfish or hake
4-5 saffron strands, crushed
Freshly-ground black pepper
2 lemons
1 bunch parsley, chopped

Wine: Most people opt for a Rosé with Paella, however we recommenda young light red wine, preferably from Valencia, as this dish tends to make one thirsty.

If possible one should cook this dish in a *paellera*., a special paella pan. They can be bought at good kitchenware shops or buy one if you are visiting Spain. The classic Valencian *paellera* is a large, round or oval, shallow iron pan with two handles. If you do not have one, you can make do with a normal large frying-pan or a wok. Seed, wash and finely chop the pepper. Peel and chop the garlic.
Cook the French beans in salted water for 10 minutes in salted water. Drain them, rinse with cold water and drain again thoroughly. Cut the stalks from the artichokes and cook

and drain them in the same way as the beans. Then cut the artichokes into small pieces, discarding the tough leaves and the chokes. Skin the tomatoes in boiling water and chop coarsely. Sprinkle the chicken pieces with salt. Heat the oil in the pan and fry the chicken and chopped pork along with the sausages and ham. Add the pepper, garlic, beans, artichokes and the sliced squid and fry on a fairly high heat.

Wash and scrape the mussels and clams and cook them in a little salted water until they open; discard any which fail to open. Strain the mussel cooking liquid through a fine sieve into a bowl and reserve for the rice.

If necessary, add some more oil to the paella pan and add the tomatoes, paprika and the snails and shrimps. Stir all the ingredients thoroughly with a large wooden spoon. Stir in the rice and peas and then arrange the pieces of fish, the mussels and clams on top. Pour about 750 ml/1½ pints of water or chicken stock over the rice mixture and add the mussel cooking liquid. Season with salt, pepper and saffron. Stir once more but from now on do not stir the dish again. Increase the heat to high then reduce it immediately and let the rice simmer for 15 minutes. If possible, put the paella into an oven preheated to 180°C/350°F/Gas Mark 4 for the last 5 minutes of cooking. Then leave it to stand for a few minutes. Slice or quarter the lemons and garnish the paella with them. Finally, sprinkle with chopped parsley and serve.

LA FIDEUA

Rice or Noodles with Fish and Shellfish.

Instead of the garlic mayonnaise, the dish can merely be served with a sprinkling of the best virgin olive oil.

375 ml/12 fl oz oil for frying	1 kg/2 lb fish fillets
500 g/1 lb shellfish	(monkfish, turbot or
of any kind	halibut)
5 garlic cloves	125-150 ml/4-8 fl oz virgin
4 small, ripe tomatoes	olive oil
60 g/2 oz blanched almonds	2 egg yolks
2 slices white bread,	1 tablespoon breadcrumbs
crusts removed, cubed	Lemon juice
3-4 strands saffron, crushed	400 g/14 oz rice or noodles
1 tablespoon Cayenne	
pepper or chilli powder	**Wine:** a light , dry or a
Salt	slightly sparkling white
2 medium-sized onions	wine such as an Albariño
500 g/1 lb potatoes	

Heat the oil in a large casserole dish and fry the shellfish. When cooked, reserve them on a plate, leaving the oil in the casserole. Peel the garlic and reserve 2 of the cloves aside. Put the tomatoes into boiling water, then skin them and chop into small pieces. Roast the almonds in a dry frying-pan, removing them as soon as they begin to give off their aroma. Then fry the following ingredients in the oil in the casserole dish, adding them to the pan in the following: garlic,tomatoes, almonds, saffron, paprika or chilli powder and bread. Season with salt and cook for about 5 minutes.

Then purée the mixture in a blender or chop them very finely. Pour the mixture back into the casserole and add 750 ml/1½ pints water. Bring slowly to the boil. Meanwhile, peel the onions and slice them into rings; peel the potatoes and cut them into cubes or slices. Wash the fish and cut it into small pieces. As soon as the sauce has come to the boil, add the onions and potatoes . Cook for 5 minutes, then add the fish and season with salt. Cook for another 10 minutes, then add the shellfish. Cook for a few minutes more, then carefully pour off the liquid into another pan.

Whilst the fish is cooking, to make the mayonnaise, put the reserved 2 cloves of garlic through a garlic crusher or chop very finely. Whisk the egg yolks in a mixing bowl with the garlic and breadcrumbs and flavour with lemon juice and salt to taste. Gradually add the olive oil, pouring it in a thin stream, and beating constantly, preferably with an electric mixer, until he mixture thickens. Place the seafood, potatoes and onions on a serving dish and cover with garlic mayonnaise.

Heat a little oil in a large saucepan and fry the rice or noodles for a few minutes. Add the reserved fish stock and cook the rice or noodles until firm but tender. Serve with the seafood stew.

TORTILLA A LA MURCIANA

Murcian Vegetable Omelette

1 onion	2 ripe tomatoes
1 sweet red pepper	6-8 eggs
120 g/4 oz cooked ham	Salt
100 ml/3½ fl oz oil	
1 courgette	**Wine:** a young red wine
1 aubergine	

Peel the onions, and seed and stem the pepper. Chop them finely along with the ham and lightly fry in the oil until golden brown in a non-stick frying pan. Peel the courgettes and aubergine, dice them and add them to the pan. Stir in all the ingredients thoroughly and continue to cook. Soak the tomatoes briefly in boiling water, skin them and chop them into small pieces . Add them to the other vegetables in the pan. Season with salt and cook for another 8-10 minutes or until the vegetables are cooked but still firm. Beat the eggs vigorously in a bowl and pour them into the vegetable mixture. Turn the heat up to high and cook on both sides until golden-brown. Flip the omelette over using a saucepan lid or large plate or if you find this too difficult finish it under a hot grill. Slide it on to a round plate to serve.

ARROZ CON COSTRA

Baked Rice

Serves 5

120 g/4 oz chick-peas
1 saveloy sausage
1 onion, peeled
and halved
1 small bay leaf
200 ml/7 fl oz oil
250 g/8 oz smoked pork
sausages (bratwurst)

1 chicken
1 garlic clove
250 ml/8 fl oz meat stock
400 g/14 oz rice
4 eggs

Wine: a full-bodied
red wine such as
Méntrida from Alicante

Soak the chick-peas overnight. Rinse them and drain them. Put the chick-peas into a large pan with the saveloy and the onion and bay leaf and add 1.5 litres/2½ pints of water. Cook until the chick-peas are tender, about 1 hour, then strain off their liquid and reserve the liquid and the chick-peas. Meanwhile, heat the oil in a large frying-pan. Slice the smoked pork sausages and cut the chicken into pieces and fry until golden-brown. Peel and finely chop the garlic, add to the pan and stir the ingredients thoroughly. Then add the meat stock and cook until the chicken is tender. Remove the sausage slices from the pan and reserve them. Pour the remaining contents of the pan into a casserole dish. Add the chick-pea cooking liquid and bring it to the boil. Meanwhile, slice the saveloy, lightly fry it in a little oil and add to the casserole. Preheat the oven to 250°C/450°F/Gas Mark 8. As soon as the contents of the casserole dish comes to the boil add the rice and chick-peas, season and stir well. Continue to cook for several minutes, then arrange the fried saveloy slices on top of the rice and chick-peas and remove from the heat. Beat the eggs in a bowl with a fork and pour them over the rice mixture. Place in the oven and cook until a golden crust forms on top. Remove from the oven and allow to stand for several minutes before serving.

ENSALADA DE HORTELANO

Mixed Salad

1 head of curly endive
200 g/7 oz carrots
200 g/7 oz chicory
240 g/8 oz pickled
gherkins
120 g/4 oz cooked
beetroot

3 celery sticks
1 onion
4 tomatoes
3 tablespoons wine
vinegar
6 tablespoons olive oil
1 bunch parsley

Wash the ingredients, dice them all and toss them in a large salad bowl or in individual salad bowls. Beat the olive oil, wine vinegar, salt, pepper and chopped parsley together to make the vinaigrette. Either pour this over the salad or serve in a vinaigrette jar.

ARROZ A LA BANDA

Fish Risotto

Serves 6

450g/1 lb potatoes
1 tablespoon oil
2 onions
Freshly-ground
black pepper
2.7 kg/6 lb fish fillets
(preferably skate or monkfish)

Salt
125 ml/4 fl oz oil
4 garlic cloves, peeled
and chopped
480 kg/1 lb rice

Wine: a full-bodied,
dry white wine such
as Alella from Rueda

Peel and cube the potatoes. Peel the onions, chop finely and fry in the oil, seasoning with a pinch of pepper. Add the potatoes and continue to fry for a while, stirring occasionally. Meanwhile, slice the fish into quite large pieces and season with salt. Arrange the fish on the potatoes and pour in enough water to cover the ingredients. Bring to the boil and cook, uncovered, for about 30 minutes, skimming off the foam as it forms. Then strain the fish cooking liquid through a sieve into another pan. Arrange the fish, potatoes and onions on a serving dish and keep warm.
Heat the oil in a saucepan and lightly brown the garlic and the rice. Add the fish broth, season with salt and simmer until the rice has absorbed all the liquid. Serve the fish, potatoes and onions on a bed of rice.

DORADA A LA SAL

Salted Sea Bream

This recipe was originally invented by the fisherman of Murcia and is now a firmly established dish on the menus of the best Spanish restaurants. The best sea bream comes from the Mediterranean, though the species has become somewhat scarce in the seas off Murcia. By preparing the fish in this way, the full flavour is brought out and no further seasoning is necessary. If sea bream is not available, other saltwater fish can be used. The difficulty with other fish is that this method of preparation often brings out a very strong flavour and the flesh tends to cook in a shorter time.

1 sea bream, weighing
approx 1 kg/2 lb
2.7 kg/6 lb sea
salt crystals

Wine: a full-bodied,
dry white wine perhaps
from La Mancha

Preheat the oven to 200°C/400°F/Gas Mark 6. Do not gut or remove scales from the sea bream. Cover the bottom of a deep oven dish with a 1 cm/½ in layer of salt. Lay the sea bream on top, cover the fish with the rest of the salt and smooth the surface. Bake in the oven for 30 minutes or until the salt becomes browned and cracked, which indicates that the fish is cooked and ready to serve.

99

The salt crust is easily removed by carefully scraping it off with a spoon. The skin will have become attached to the salt crust, so the fish will be ready to eat.

GUISADO DE TRIGO

Corn and Chick-pea Soup

This purely vegetarian stew originates from the kingdom of Murcia and was traditionally eaten on Maundy Thursday. It has been rediscovered as a culinary delight.

300 g/10 oz chick-peas
300 g/10 oz dried
 corn kernels
280 g/1 lb potatoes
480 g//1 lb French beans
250 g/8 oz pumpkin,
skinned and diced
1 medium-sized onion
1 ripe tomato

2 tablespoons oil
3 saffron strands
1 fresh mint sprig
Salt
Pepper

Wine: a young red wine such as Almansa from La Mancha.

Soak the chick-peas and corn kernels overnight, changing the water from time to time. Boil the chick-peas in a large pot in plenty of water, until almost soft, about 45 minutes. Meanwhile peel the potatoes, dice them and add them to the pot with the chick-peas along with the corn, French beans and the pumpkin. Chop the onions finely. Dip the tomatoes in hot water then skin and chop them finely . Brown the onions in the oil then add the tomatoes and cook briefly. Add this mixture to the pot, stir, and season with the saffron, chopped mint, salt and freshly ground pepper. Simmer gently until all the ingredients are cooked, about 30 minutes.

CORDERO LECHAL AL ESTILO DE MURCIA

Murcian-style Stuffed Legs of Lamb

4 legs of suckling lamb
(weighing about
 480 g/1 lb)
100 g/3½ oz pork
dripping or lard
1 large onion
2 bay leaves
1 small sprig thyme
1 ripe tomato
1 bottle white wine
(0.7 litres)
600 ml/1 pint meat stock
6 medium-sized
cooking apples

16 small potatoes
1 tablespoon
pine kernels
2 garlic cloves
1 bunch parsley
Salt
Freshly-ground
black pepper

Wine: a mature vintage red wine (*de reserva*) such as Priorato

Ask your butcher to dress the lamb legs and to chop the bone into small pieces. Put the lard in a large saucepan, reserving 2 teaspoons of it in a cup. Peel and roughly chop the onions and add them with the lamb bones, bay leaves, thyme and the finely-chopped tomatoes to the saucepan. Gently fry on a low heat for 15 minutes. Turn the heat up to high, pour in the wine and reduce to a third of its original volume. Add the meat stock and cook for a further 5 minutes. Then strain the sauce through a conical sieve into a bowl and reserve it.

Season the legs of lamb inside and out with salt and freshly ground black pepper and rub the remaining lard into them. Peel, quarter and core the apples. Fill each leg with 6 pieces of apple, roll them up and close the edges with toothpicks. Arrange the stuffed legs in an ovenproof dish.

Preheat the oven to 220°C/425°F/Gas Mark 7. Peel the potatoes and arrange them around the legs of lamb. Peel the garlic and cut it into slices. Wash and finely chop the parsley. Sprinkle the pine kernels, garlic and chopped parsley over the lamb. Pour the strained sauce over the lamb and place in the preheated oven. When a golden-brown crust forms on the lamb, the dish is ready to serve.

ARRÒS AMB FESOLS I NAPS

Rice with Turnips and Broad Beans

If fresh pig's ears and trotters are not available, use salted or pickled ones and soak them for 24 hours in fresh water.

Salt	4 blood sausages
250 g/8 oz broad beans	400 g/14 oz rice
6 small turnips	2-3 saffron strands
400 g/14 oz ham hocks	
200 g/7 oz pig's ear	**Wine:** a young red wine
1 small pig's trotter	such as from Ampurdán in
120 g/4 oz smoked bacon	La Mancha

Soak the beans overnight. Drain them and discard the soaking water. Bring 3 litres/5½ pints of salted water to the boil in a large saucepan. Drain the beans and rinse them. Wash the turnips and slice them. Add the beans, turnips, pork and the blood sausage and simmer until tender. Then remove the pork and sausage, allow to cool and cut into small pieces. Season the broth to taste and add the saffron. Add the rice and simmer on a low heat for about 30 minutes until cooked, adding the offal and sausage after 15 minutes. The dish is cooked when the rice is tender but not too dry. It should have a slightly mushy consistency. If necessary add more water.

SORBETE DE NARANJA

Orange Sorbet

Serves 6	150 g/5 oz sugar
	30 ml/1 fl oz brandy
About 4 unpeeled oranges	or Campari

Wash the oranges and peel the rind extremely thinly, into thin strips so that no pith. A potato peeler is good for this purpose. Bring 375 ml/12 fl oz water to the boil in a saucepan with the sugar. Add the orange peel and simmer for a further 10-15 minutes.

Meanwhile squeeze the juice from the oranges and reserve it. You will need 500 ml/17 fl oz of juice, so use more oranges if necessary. Strain the orange peel syrup through a fine sieve into a mixing bowl. Stir the alcohol into the mixture and allow to cool. Then mix the orange juice into the syrup. Freeze the sorbet mixture for at least 3 hours. Remove it and stir the sorbet at least twice to break down the ice crystals, so that it freezes smoothly and does not become too solid.

NEW CASTILE, MADRID, ESTREMADURA

Authentic New Castilian food is hearty, peasant fare. The dishes here are simple and traditional. The plains of La Mancha stretch endlessly across into the south-eastern part of New Castile where borders are not clearly defined and, food is cooked simply. It consists mainly of hearty soups eaten with fried flatbread and lamb stews. Several game dishes whose main ingredients are partridge and wild rabbit are also firmly established on the local menu. The extensive hunting grounds of New Castile provide its kitchens with everything, and the chefs and housewives willingly cook whatever the hunters shoot and bring back with them.

Even in Madrid, the residents seem to prefer cooking and eating simple food. Madrid is now the capital of Spain, so one can find every kind of authentically prepared food from around the world. Fortunately, a few traditional dishes continue to remain favourites in the midst of cosmopolitan influences and these are known to be purely and authentically Spanish. They include cocido madrileño (a hearty stew), callos a la madrileña (Tripe Madrid-style and judias del tío Lucas" (a stew containing haricot beans, plenty of garlic and bacon). Madrid is also the home of the world-famous thick omelette with potatoes known as tortilla de patatas.

Overleaf: Windmills and castle ruins.

Below left: The "hanging houses" of Cuenca, precariously poised over the valley.

The monastery and convent kitchens are responsible for shaping Estremadura's culinary history. The monasteries of Yuste, Guadalupe and Alcantara are famous in Spain for their expertise which has heavily influenced regional cooking . By today's standards, the style of cooking is extremely simple. But then Estremadura is an unusual and very poor region with a lonely landscape dotted with small towns. The meat of the goats and lambs which graze on the wild highlands and is used extensively in local cooking.

Left: The underground wine cellars of La Mancha are rather inconspicuous.

Below: The wine is stored in gigantic clay vats during the fermentation process.

Game

In the days of the Roman Empire, Spain was known for its extremely large grain harvest and was called "the Roman granary". Today, one could call Spain and especially the provinces of New Castile and Estremadura, could be called "the hunting grounds of Europe".

Estremadura, New Castile and Albacete have the largest highland and lowland hunting grounds in Spain, where there are plenty of partridges and native Spanish game birds such as the redcock (*Alectoris rufus)* are abundant. The rabbit used to be the most popular game to hunt, but when the mixamatosis epidemic spread from France to Spain, the rabbit population went into a decline. It has never regained its former size. The rabbit, which originates from North Africa, was so popular in Spain in ancient times that the poet Catullus described Spain as the "*cuniculosa Celtiberia*", the Celtic Iberia of rabbits. Today one might say the same as regards partridges. Small game hunters from all over the world come to Spain to hunt partridges.

There are also many other lowland game to be found, apart from the partridge, including hare, quail, woodcock, ducks and the olive-fattened thrush.

The wild boar is the commonest large game animal in all the regions of Spain. Various varieties of deer are confined

Facing page below left: There is still an abundance of wild boar in Estremadura and La Mancha.

Below: There's good game shooting for the hunters of New Castile and Estremadura.

mainly to the well maintained Castilian hunting reserves. During the hunting season about two million people wander the mountains and plains in search of prey. Hunters maintain that the preliminaries of the hunt are just as much fun as the kill so they set out with an old Spanish saying:

"De la liebre y el cielo lo que le da el sol,
y de la perdiz, lo que le da la sombra"

which loosely translated means:

"The best part of hare and rabbits is the back and of the partridge it is the breast".

TORTILLA DE PATATAS

Potato Omelette

Spain is famous for its *tortillas.* There are many recipes using this technique for cooking eggs. *Tortilla de patatas* is cooked throughout Spain. Sometimes it includes onions or even tomatoes, and it is served either in small pieces as a *tapas* (pre-dinner snacks) or as a main course. It tastes just as good cold as hot.

1 kg/2½ lb potatoes	**Wine:** any wine goes
250 ml/8 fl oz olive oil	well with tortillas, except
8 eggs	sweet white wine
Salt	

Peel and wash the potatoes, dry them with kitchen paper and cut them into thick slices. Heat two-thirds of the oil in a round frying-pan and cook the potatoes, covered, on a low heat for 15 minutes or until they are soft. Remove the lid, increase the heat and briefly fry the potatoes until they are golden-brown. Drain any remaining oil from the pan. Beat the eggs vigorously in a bowl and stir the potatoes into the eggs. .Season well with salt and pepper and leave to stand for 15 minutes. Heat the remaining oil in the pan on a high heat. Add the egg-and-potato mixture, pat it down and leave to cook for a few minutes. Then flip the omelette over with the help of a large saucepan lid or flat plate and cook the other side until golden-brown.

GRATINADO DE BERENJENAS

Aubergine Gratin

4 large aubergines	1 sprig fresh basil
50 g/2 oz flour	Salt
200 ml/7 fl oz olive oil	60 g/2 oz Emmental or
1 kg/2 lb ripe tomatoes	Parmesan cheese, freshly
1 clove garlic	grated
½ teaspoon dried basil or	

Cut the aubergines lengthways into thick slices and dip them in flour. Heat the oil in a large frying-pan over a brisk flame and fry the aubergines on both sides until golden-brown. Drain them on kitchen paper. Preheat the oven to 200°C/400°F/Gas Mark 6. Dip the tomatoes in hot water, skin them and strain them through a sieve. Combine the tomato purée with the peeled garlic, and grind them together in a blender. Season with basil and salt. Arrange the browned aubergine slices in a shallow ovenproof dish, covering each layer with some of the tomato purée. Sprinkle with the grated cheese and bake for 20 minutes. Serve hot.

COCIDO MADRILENO

Madrid Boiled Dinner

Cocido madrileño is the pride of Madrid cuisine and has become an extremely popular dish. However, it takes so long to prepare that it is rarely cooked in these hectic times. Originally, it consisted of three courses - a soup flavoured with mint, a dish of chick peas, potatoes and other vegetables, followed by a dish of assorted kinds of meat and sausages. At the beginning of this century, *cocido madrileño* was simplified by the invention of the small Madrid soup bowl. This enabled construction workers to carry the dish from home to the building site, where they would heat it up over a wood fire. All that is history now. Today the dish is a culinary treat, served with great pomp and ceremony in Madrid's' finest restaurants. If ox is not available, use beef.

Serves 6

480 g/1 lb chick-peas
½ pickled pig's trotter
1 smoked pigs' ear
480 g/1 lb ox (rump or shoulder)
1 ox bone
120 g/4 oz smoked bacon
120 g/4 oz raw ham (Serrano ham if possible)
1 carrot
1 small turnip
1 stick celery
1 small onion peeled and spiked with a clove

½ chicken
Salt
6 medium-sized potatoes
Pepper
1 large white cabbage
60 g/2 oz French beans
1 chorizo sausage
1 blood sausage
2-3 tablespoons oil
1 clove garlic, peeled and sliced
75 g/2½ oz noodles or rice

Wine: a young red wine such as Ribeiro from Tarragona

Soak the chick-peas with the pig's trotter and ear in cold water for 12 hours. Drain and discard the water.
Boil the ox meat, and bone, pig's trotter and ear, smoked bacon and raw ham together in a large pan in 3 litres/5½ pints water. As the water boils, skim the foam off the top with a slotted- spoon. Coarsely chop the carrot , turnip and celery. Add these vegetables to the pan along with the chick peas, onion, chicken and 1 teaspoon salt. Simmer on a low heat until tender. Peel and cube the potatoes and add them 15 minutes before the end of the cooking time. Season with pepper and more salt to taste.
Meanwhile, wash and clean the cabbage, chop it roughly and place in another saucepan with the sausages. Cover with water, bring to the boil, then simmer until tender. Drain the liquid from the cabbage and reserve the vegetables and sausages in a bowl. Heat the oil in a frying-pan and quickly brown the garlic on high heat for 3 minutes, then add the reserved vegetables. Reserve the mixture again in a warm place.
To make the soup, pour any remaining cooking liquid from the chick-peas and pork into a saucepan. Bring to the boil and add the noodles or rice. Coarsely chop all the meat from the first pan. place the drained chick-peas on a large serving dish, followed by the ox and chicken meat, the ham and smoked bacon, and finally the pigs' offal on top. Pour the noodle or rice soup into a large soup-tureen. Slice the chorizo and the blood sausage and arrange the vegetables on a second serving dish, topped with the sausages and potatoes.

CALLOS A LA MADRILEÑA

Madrid-style Tripe

600 g/1½ lb calves' tripe
1 calf's foot
Vinegar
1 bouquet garni
500 ml/17 fl oz white wine
1 medium-sized onion studded with 2 cloves
2 leeks
100 g/3½ oz pork dripping or lard
120 g/4 oz raw ham (preferably Serrano ham)
90 g/3 oz chorizo

1 tablespoon paprika
3 tomatoes
2 small dried chillies, stalks and seeds removed
1 tablespoon flour
Salt
Pepper
1 bunch parsley, chopped

Wine: a strong red wine such as Penedès from Rioja

Wash the tripe and calf's foot. Cut the tripe into cubes or thick strips and the calf's foot into 4 pieces. Soak in water to which vinegar has been added (60 ml/2 fl oz vinegar to 1 litre/1¾ pints of water) for 15 minutes, then rinse with cold water. Bring plenty of water to the boil in a large saucepan and add the tripe and foot along with the bouquet garni and wine and simmer for about 4 hours, or until the tripe is tender. Allow to cool. Meanwhile, wash and clean the carrots and leeks and chop them very finely. Take the tripe and foot out of the pot and place them in another pot with the leeks, carrots and onion. Keep warm. Reserve the stock. Heat the lard in a pan and briefly brown the diced ham and the sliced chorizo. Season with the paprika, then add to the pan with the meat.
Steep the tomatoes in boiling water, remove the skins and purée them or chop them finely. Add the tomatoes to the frying-pan with the halved chillies and the flour. Stir well and cook over medium heat. Add a ladleful of the veal stock, cook for a few minutes more, then strain through a sieve over the tripe. Season with salt and pepper, stir and simmer on a low heat for another hour. Sprinkle with chopped parsley before serving.

GALLINA EN PEPITORIA

Chicken in Almond Sauce

Serves 6

1 large, oven-ready chicken
Salt
Pepper
Flour
4 tablespoons oil
1 large onion
1 tablespoon oil
300 ml/10 fl oz dry white wine

1.5 litres/2½ pints chicken stock
1 bay leaf
1 small sprig thyme
2 hard-boiled egg yolks
150 g/5 oz blanched almonds

Wine: a young red wine such as Ribera del Duero

Divide the chicken into 8 pieces, season with salt and pepper, coat in flour and fry in 3 tablespoons oil until golden-brown. Remove the chicken from the pan and drain it well on kitchen paper. Peel and chop the onions. Add the remaining oil to the pan and fry the onions until they are transparent, then stir in a tablespoon of flour and cook for 1 minute. Add the wine and stir well for a few minutes. Purée the sauce in a blender or pass it through a sieve. Place the chicken in a casserole dish, add the chicken stock, the herbs and the onion sauce. Stir well and bring to the boil on a high heat. Reduce the heat and simmer for about 1 hour.

Mash the hard-boiled egg yolks with a fork. Chop the almonds and roast them briefly under a hot grill. Mix the egg yolks and almonds together and garnish the chicken with it before serving. Accompany with rice.

GAZPACHO PASTORIL

Country Gazpacho

Serves 6

1 oven-ready rabbit,
preferably wild, with offal
1 oven-ready partridge,
with offal
450 ml/15 fl oz olive oil
1 bulb of garlic, trimmed
Water

2 Tomatoes
1 sweet green or
 red pepper, seeded
 and finely chopped
4 slices crispbread
Salt

Wine: a young red
wine such as a Valdepeñas
from Valencia

Wash the rabbit and partridge offal and chop them into large pieces . Season with salt. Heat two-thirds of the oil in a casserole dish and brown the whole bulb of garlic. When it is browned, add enough water to cover the meat and continue to cook on a low heat. Steep the tomatoes in boiling water, skin them and chop them into small pieces. Fry the tomatoes and pepper in a pan in the remaining oil and add them to the casserole. Crush the crispbread into crumbs and add them to the pot. Continue to cook until the birds are tender and the juice has thickened. Season to taste and serve hot.

PISTO MANCHEGO

Vegetable Stew "a la Mancha"

1 large onion
2 sweet red peppers,
seeded
4 potatoes, peeled
2 medium-sized
courgettes
4 ripe tomatoes
60 g/2 oz smoked bacon
75 g/2½ oz pork dripping

or lard
250 ml/8 fl oz meat stock
Salt
Pepper

Wine: a young red wine
such as a Tarragona
from La Mancha

Peel and chop the onions. Dice the peppers and the potatoes. Cut the courgettes into thick slices. Steep the tomatoes in boiling water, skin them and cut them into small pieces. Dice the bacon.
Heat half the lard in a large, deep frying-pan and cook the onions and bacon until golden-brown. Add the potatoes and courgettes, stir carefully and cook slowly until soft. Heat the remainder of the lard in a second pan and cook the tomatoes and peppers. Then add these to the first pan. Add the stock, season with salt and pepper and cook, uncovered, until the stock has reduced by half.

BESUGO A LA MADRILEÑA

Red Sea Bream Madrid-style

2 tomatoes	2 lemons
100 ml/3½ fl oz oil	3 garlic cloves
Salt	1 small bunch parsley
Freshly ground	60 g/2 oz breadcrumbs
black pepper	175 ml/6 fl oz white wine
1 bay leaf	
1 red sea bream,	**Wine:** a robust vintage
weighing approx	white wine such as Cava,
1 kg/2½ lb,	Granvás
cleaned and gutted	

Steep the tomatoes in boiling water, skin them and sieve them. Purée the tomatoes. Heat half the oil in a pan, add the tomato purée and the bay leaf and season with salt and pepper. Simmer for 5 minutes. Discard the bay leaf and reserve the sauce.

Wash the sea bream and dry thoroughly inside and out with kitchen paper. Score the fish lightly in several places on the skin. Sprinkle the whole fish with the juice of 1 lemon. Cut the other lemon into thick slices and place them in the slits made by the score marks. Leave the fish to marinate in the lemons for 30 minutes. Meanwhile, peel the garlic and chop finely along with the washed parsley. Mix them in a bowl with the breadcrumbs.

Preheat the oven to 150°C/300°F/Gas Mark 2. Heat the remainder of the oil in a flat, ovenproof dish and arrange the fish in it. Brush the fish with the oil and place it in the oven. After 5 minutes, add half the wine and after a further 5 minutes add the tomato sauce. Sprinkle with the breadcrumb mixture , season with salt and freshly ground pepper then add the rest of the wine. Bake the fish until tender about 45 minutes.

Remove the fish to a serving dish. Before serving, reheat the sauce in a saucepan. Remove the lemon slices from the fish and pour the sauce over the fish

TOCINO DE CIELO

Heavenly Soufflés

300 g/10 oz sugar	12 egg yolks
1 vanilla pod or	Individual soufflé dishes
1 cinnamon stick	

Boil the sugar, with the vanilla pod or cinnamon stick with 250 ml/8 fl oz water in a saucepan until it becomes a thick syrup. It is ready as soon as one can draw threads from it with a wooden spoon. Allow to cool. Spread a little of the syrup on the bottom of the soufflé dishes. Vigorously beat the egg yolks in a mixing bowl. Strain the syrup through a fine sieve, stir it into the egg yolks and fill the soufflé dishes with the mixture.

Preheat the oven to 130°C/275°F/Gas Mark 3. Place the soufflé dishes in an oven tin filled with water; the water should reach only half-way up the sides of the soufflé dishes. Bake them in the oven for 20 minutes., ensuring that the water does not boil away and spray over the dishes, or the egg mixture will not solidify.

TORRIJAS

Poor Knights

500 ml/17 fl oz milk	About 2 tablespoons
150 g/5 oz sugar	ground cinnamon
8 slices of white bread	
about 1.5 cm/½ in thick	**Wine:** a heavy, vintage
1 egg	dessert wine such as a
250 ml/8 fl oz oil	sweet sherry or a Malaga
	wine

Gently warm the milk and stir in half the sugar. Soak the slices of bread in the mixture and remove, them one by one, then gently squeeze them, allowing them to retain their shape. Beat the eggs vigorously and dip the bread slices in them. Heat the oil in a frying-pan and fry the bread on both sides until golden-brown. Arrange it on a plate, sprinkle with sugar and ground cinnamon and serve hot.

TARTE DE VAINILLA

Vanilla Cake

75 g/2½ oz bitter	
(cooking) chocolate	50g/1 oz butter, softened
50 g/1¾ oz candied	200 g/7 oz marzipan
lemon peel	80 g/2 ¾ oz sugar
60 g/2 oz ground almonds	Pulp from 2 vanilla pods
80 g/2¾ oz flour	5 eggs, separated
40g/1½ oz bicarbonate	70 g/2¾ oz sugar
of soda	200 g/7 oz apricot jam

Chop the chocolate coarsely into medium-sized pieces and mix thoroughly with the candied lemon peel, ground almonds, flour and bicarbonate of soda in a bowl.

Crumble the marzipan and knead it with the butter in another bowl. Add the sugar, vanilla and egg yolks, one after the other and mix in thoroughly. Then whip the egg whites into stiff peaks and fold them in, followed by the chocolate mixture. Preheat the oven to 190°C/375°F/Gas Mark 5. Place the mixture in a cake tin lined with greaseproof paper, level the top with a palette knife and bake in the oven on the second shelf for 45 minutes.

Remove the cake from the oven, allow it to cool for 10 minutes and remove the cake from the tin. Gently heat the apricot jam until it thins, then pour it through a sieve and brush it on the top and sides of the cake. When it has dried, ice the cake with chocolate and decorate to taste.

ANDALUSIA

*F*iestas and Flamencos, dangerous bullfights and beautiful horses are only part of the attraction of Andalusia. This is the most heavily-populated part of Spain, a province the size of Portugal with a colourful, varied past. Andalusia has been invaded in turn by the Phoenicians, the Western Goths, the Romans and the Moors, all of whom have influenced and shaped its culture. The Arab influence remains strong, even in the cuisine. The Andalusian climate, particularly the hot summers and the proximity of the Mediterranean and Atlantic are also factors which contribute to the diet. Here too, there is a speciality, which is also popular in neighbouring provinces,. It is gazpacho, *a cold soup which comes in many different combinations, made either with plenty of raw, finely chopped vegetables or as* gazpacho blanco cordobés, *with apples, or the sweet soup of grapes and Málaga wine known as* ajoblanco de Málaga.

*A*ndalusians are experts in the preparation of egg dishes. Apparently the best huevos fritos *(fried eggs) come from Seville. The yolks are supposed to taste best and the whites are the crispest, so it is said. It is considered a disgrace for someone to order a single fried egg and so, if only for the sake of appearances, several are eaten at once. Furthermore, there are* huevos revueltos (*plain omelettes*), tortillas (*thick omelettes, often containing a vegetable mixture*) *and* huevos flamencos, *eggs cooked the gypsy way with chorizo and vegetables. Andalusian cuisine also offers a range of fish and seafood dishes, including* abaja de Algeciras , *a fish soup,* soldaditos de Pavia (*cod fillets in batter*), panojas malagueñas (*anchovies in butter*), las sardinas de Málaga (*sardines Málaga-style*), la coquina (*large mussels*), el pescadito frito gaditano *and* los chanquetes (*whitebait fried in oil*). *Not forgetting* las bocas de la Isla (*large crab claws*), el barbo encebollado (*red mullet with onion*), los chocos de Huelva (*squid*), el rape con patatas" (*monkfish with potatoes*) *and* la pesca de la malagueña (*hake Malaga-style*).

Overleaf: Landscape in the Sierra Nevada around Doña Maria.

Below left: Sherry is delivered from the cask to the glass in this flamboyant manner.

*S*ince the finest sherry comes from Andalusia, specifically from the town of Jeréz, it is not only drunk but also used for cooking. A fine example of this is pigs' kidneys *al Jerez, Other types of offal such as tripe is also popular. Partridges are prepared* a la torero, *stuffed with ham and anchovy fillets. There is an excellent recipe from Granada using cured ham from Trevelez, the highest village in Spain. Raw cured ham, similar to prosciutto, is a famous Spanish delicacy, its proper name is* jamon serrano. *Another speciality of the region is* toro, *meat from a bull, killed in a bullfight.*

T he Arab influence is quite pronounced when it comes to desserts. There is a large and irresistable array of dulcerias, *sweet pastries. An example of these are* polverones sevillanos, *shortcrust pastries which melt in the mouth*.

Left: The Andalusian women still store their water the traditional way in earthenware pitchers.

Page 121 below: "El Rocio", the most famous religious procession in Spain.

Olive Oil

Olive oil plays a crucial role in the Spanish kitchen as salad oil or for frying. In the 18th and 19th centuries, fried dishes were particularly popular and unimaginable without olive oil.

It takes seven years for an olive tree to bear fruit and the longer the olives hang from the branches, the darker they become. Green olives are harvested from November onwards and the violet, almost black fruits are ready by January or February. For the best olive oil , the so-called extra-virgin olive oil, *oleo extra vérgine*, unripe olives are used in the first pressing.

There are still a multitude of recipes for foods fried in olive oil. In Andalusia there are even desserts which include cold pressed olive oil among the ingredients, such as *las torrijas* (poor knights), *los canutillos* (puff pastry rolls), *la leche frita* (custard squares fried in olive oil), *los buñuelos* (fritters), *los churros* (fried pastries) and *las hojuelas andaluz*, Andalusian deep-fried honey cakes.

The olives for the oil are harvested in Catalonia, Valencia, Aragon and of course, Andalusia. These olive-producing regions are known as *zonas de fritos*, areas of fried food, of which Adalusia is the leader.

Top right: The olives are beaten from the trees with sticks.

Right facing: Olives are still gathered laboriously by hand.

Below: Some of the olive trees are as old as 2000 years.

GAZPACHO ANDALUZ

Andalusian Chilled Vegetable Soup

There are two types of *gazpacho* in Spain, the *gazpacho manchego* from La Mancha, which is cooked in a frying pan with game. and *el gazpacho andaluz*, a chilled vegetable soup. Whilst the *gazpacho manchego* is probably an older recipe, *gazpacho andaluz* enjoys international popularity. Both are served with bread. The word *gazpacho* originates from the Latin caspa, which means something like "little pieces", referring to the pieces of bread used in both dishes.

Serves 6	1 slice white bread, crusts removed
1 sweet red pepper	250 ml/8 fl oz olive oil
1 sweet green pepper	250 ml/8 fl oz wine vinegar
8 ripe tomatoes	Salt
2 small cucumbers	Chopped vegetables and
2 cloves garlic	fried bread cubes to garnish.

Seed the peppers and slice them in half. Steep the tomatoes briefly in boiling water and skin them. Peel the cucumbers. Chop all the vegetables coarsely. Peel the garlic and put it in a blender with the vegetables. Tear the bread into pieces and add it to the blender with the olive oil, salt and 250 ml/8 fl oz water. Liquidise to a purée. If some pieces still remain, pass them through a sieve with a little water. Put the soup in the fridge, serve cold and accompany with finely diced tomatoes, cucumbers, peppers, onion and fried bread cubes.

ABAJÁ DE ALGECIRAS

Algeciran-style Fish Soup

1 kg/2 lb fish fillets, cut into bite-sized pieces	3 slices white bread, crusts removed
Salt	A few strands saffron
125 ml/4 floz dry white wine	5 black peppercorns
¾ onion	450 ml/15 fl oz olive oil
6 garlic cloves	
1 small bunch parsley	**Wine:** a full-bodied white
Oil for frying	wine such as Rueda from
1 medium-sized tomato	Campo de Borja

Wash the fish, dry it with kitchen paper and cut it into medium-sized pieces. Cook them in 1 litre/1½ pints of salted water. As soon as the water comes to the boil, add the white wine.
Peel the onion and 1 of the garlic cloves. Chop them finely with the parsley and fry in one third of the oil in a large saucepan until golden-brown. Steep the tomatoes in boiling water, skin them, chop them and add them to the pan. Then add about 45m ml/15 fl oz of the fish cooking liquid. Crumble the bread, add it to the pan, mix everything thoroughly and cook on low heat. for 5 minutes. Put the saffron, 1 peeled garlic clove and the peppercorns in a mortar and crush them with a pestle. Stir in a few drops of olive oil and a little fish stock, then add the mixture to the pan. Simmer for 10 minutes, then pour the soup into a tureen and keep it warm. Put the fish in a saucepan and cook on a low heat with 4 cloves crushed garlic, the rest of the oil and some more fish stock. Cook for 10 minutes. Pour the fish and its sauce into the soup. Carefully reheat the soup, without letting it come to the boil, and serve.

AJOBLANCO DE MÁLAGA

Garlic Soup with Grapes

About 120 ml/4 fl oz milk
200 g/7 oz white bread, crusts removed
200 g/7 oz blanched almonds
4 garlic cloves
250 ml/8 fl oz cold pressed olive oil
Salt
Vinegar
250 g/8 oz muscatel grapes

Soak the bread in a little milk, then squeeze dry. Blend the almonds, the peeled garlic and soaked bread in a mixer, then slowly blend in the oil, followed by 1 litre/1¾ pints of water. Season with salt and a little vinegar. Serve cold, garnished with seeded or seedless grapes.

RIÑONES AL JEREZ

Veal Kidneys in Sherry Sauce

4 veal kidneys
Salt
150 ml/10 fl oz oil
1 onion
1 bunch parsley

125 ml/4 fl oz sherry (fino
or medium dry)

Wine: A red wine, such as
one from Jumilla

Wash the kidneys, cut them into thick slices and soak them in salted water for 3 hours. Chop the onions and parsley finely. Heat the oil in a frying-pan and fry them until golden brown. Add the veal kidneys, season with salt and pepper and fry on a high heat for 2 minutes. Add the sherry, stir well and cook for another 30 seconds. Serve immediately.

HABAS A LA GRANADINA

Broad Beans with Eggs

1 kg/2 lb fresh (or frozen)
broad beans
12 small artichokes
(or canned artichoke hearts
in salt water)
200 ml/7 fl oz oil
1 bunch spring onions
1 clove garlic
1 bunch mixed
herbs (bay leaf, mint
and parsley)

½ tablespoon caraway
seeds
3 peppercorns
4 small pieces white
bread
4 tablespoons vegetable
stock
Salt
4-8 eggs

Wine: a young red wine

Cook the broad beans in boiling salted water for a few minutes. Meanwhile, wash the artichokes and remove the hard outer leaves. If canned artichoke hearts are used, drain off the salted water. Drain the cooking water from the beans and put the beans and artichokes in a casserole dish. Chop the spring onions and peeled garlic finely and fry them until golden-brown in half the oil. Add them along with the bunch of herbs to the pot containing the vegetables. Add enough water to the pot to cover the vegetables and bring to the boil. Cover the pot with a lid, reduce the heat slightly and cook until the vegetables are tender, about 10 minutes.

Preheat the oven to 200°C/400°F/Gas Mark 6. Whilst the vegetables are cooking, fry the slices of bread in the remaining oil. Allow them to cool a little, then

grind them in a mortar and stir in a little vegetable stock to get a fairly thick consistency. Season with salt and stir the bread purée into the vegetables. Crack 1-2 eggs per person on top of the soup, place the soup in the oven and cook until the egg whites solidify.

PINCHITO MORUNO

Chicken and Lamb Kebabs

300 g/10 oz chicken breasts	4 tablespoons oil
500 g/1 lb lean lamb	1 tablespoon salt
1 sweet green pepper	Freshly-ground black
1 sweet red pepper	pepper
8 shallots	
4 bay leaves	**Wine:** a young red wine

Cut the chicken breast and lamb into equal-sized thick chunks. Seed and wash the peppers and cut them into medium-sized squares. Peel the shallots and cut them in half if they are too large. Put everything into a bowl and cover with the oil. Season with salt and pepper and mix well. Preheat the grill to high. Meanwhile, stick the pieces on skewer in the following order: shallot, chicken, green or red pepper, lamb, green or red pepper, bay leaf, green or red pepper and so on, finishing each skewer with a shallot. Lay the skewers on a trivet or in the grill pan to catch the fat and cook for 10 minutes on a high heat, turning from time to time. Alternatively, the kebabs can be barbecued .
If you use wooden skewers, soak them in water first to prevent burning.

GUISO DE RABO DE TORO

Stewed Bull's Tail with Potatoes

Bull's tail is unlikely to be available outside Spain, in which case use oxtail.

Serves 6

4 kg/9 lb tail of young bull
2 kg/4½ lb onions
375 ml/12 fl oz oil
1 kg/2 lb tomatoes
2 cloves garlic
½ teaspoon powdered saffron
Pepper
750 ml/1½ pints dry white wine or fino sherry
1 kg/2 lb potatoes

Wine: a good quality vintage red wine (*de reserva*)

Cut the tail into pieces at the joints . Peel the onions, chop them finely and brown them in half the oil in a large casserole dish. Steep the tomatoes in boiling water, skin and cut them into quarters. Add the pieces of bull's tail, the tomatoes and the peeled garlic. Season with saffron and pepper and fry until browned, stirring occasionally. Add the wine, cover the pan and simmer slowly on a low heat for about 2 hours. Meanwhile, peel the potatoes, cut them into thick slices and fry until golden-brown in the remaining oil. Add the potatoes to the casserole in the last half hour of the cooking time. Remove the casserole from the heat when potatoes are done. This dish tastes best if refrigerated for 8-10 hours, and reheated before serving.

CALLOS A LA ANDALUZA

Tripe with Chick-peas

Serves 8

480 g/1 lb chick-peas
4 kg/3 lb veal chitterlings
4 kg/3 lb veal towel tripe
3 small calves' feet
1 litre/1¾ pints wine vinegar
4 lemons, juice squeezed
1 onion
8 garlic cloves
1 tablespoon paprika
1 bunch of mixed herbs (parsley, mint and rosemary)
1 large bone (preferably pork)
Salt
4 chorizo sausages
1 blood sausage
2 sweet green peppers
200 g/7 oz tomatoes
2 tablespoons oil
100 g/3 ½ oz diced Serrano ham
½ teaspoon nutmeg
A few saffron strands

Wine: a young red wine, perhaps from la Mancha

Soak the chick-peas overnight. Wash the chitterlings and tripe and scrape away excess fat with a knife. Cut into small strips and place in a large bowl. Split the calves' feet, in half, cut them into small pieces and add to the offal. Pour the half the vinegar and half the lemon juice over them and mix well by hand. Leave to stand for 20 minutes and drain. Repeat this cleaning procedure in a second bowl with the remaining vinegar and lemon juice, then rinse three or four times, until the offal is thoroughly clean and odourless.

Put the offal in a large saucepan, cover with water and boil for 1 hour. Then thoroughly rinse and drain the chick-peas. Peel the onion and 5 cloves of garlic and chop finely. Add the herbs and the bone, the chick-peas, onion, garlic and paprika to the pan of offal . Add enough water to cover the ingredients. Season generously with salt and continue to cook until the offal is tender. Add the chorizo and blood sausages and cook for a further 15 minutes. Remove the bone from the pot , cut the meat from it and return the meat to the pan. Seed the peppers and slice them diagonally into thin strips. Steep the tomatoes in boiling water, skin them and chop into small pieces. Heat the oil in a frying pan and brown the peppers, tomatoes and diced ham, then mix these into the offal. Roughly chop the remaining 3 garlic cloves and grind them in a mortar with the saffron and nutmeg. Dilute with a little cooking liquid from the pot , then add this mixture to the pot. Finally, season with salt and simmer for a while longer. Shortly before serving, remove the bunch of herbs and the sausages. Slice the sausages, arrange them on a serving-dish and serve them with the stewed tripe.

SOLDADITOS DE PAVÍA

Little Soldiers from Pavia

These cod puffs were named, not after the Italian town, but after the colours of the uniforms worn by the Hussar regiments formed in Pavia, royal blue trousers and saffron-yellow-and-red tunics.

1 small piece dried cod
6 saffron strands
2 garlic cloves
1 teaspoon caraway seeds
2 tablespoons flour
240g/1 lb sifted flour
2 tablespoons vinegar
Salt
Water
1 small bunch parsley
2-3 tablespoons oil
3 egg whites
125 ml/4 fl oz oil
1 lemon, to garnish

Wine: a full-bodied white wine

Soak the dried cod for 24 hours, changing the water several times. At the end of the soaking time, drain it, discarding the soaking water and chop it very finely. Pound the saffron with the peeled garlic and the caraway seeds in a mortar and mix well with 2 tablespoons of the flour. Sift the rest of the flour again, and add the vinegar, ½ teaspoon of salt, a few tablespoons of water and the saffron paste in a food processor until it becomes a thick dough. Bind the cod with a few drops of oil and mix in to the dough. Whisk the egg whites into stiff peaks and fold into the dough. Heat the oil in a frying-pan and fry teaspoon-sized pieces of the cod mixture on both sides. Arrange them on a plate and decorate with slices of lemon.

POLVERONES

Cinnamon Crisps

Andalusian sweets have been famous throughout Spain for hundreds of years. This ancient tradition is founded upon the early availability of honey and sugar cane, cultivated in the Motril region of this part of southern pain. It is also interesting to note that many of these sweets have names connected with religion, such as *suspiros de monja*-(Nun's sighs), *cabellos de angel* (Angel's hair), *lenguas de obispo* (Bishop's tongues), and so on. The names originate from the convent bakeries, and the cakes and sweetmeats were intended to encourage religious inspiration.

These cinnamon biscuits also have a long Hispano-Arab tradition. A distinctive feature of Andalusian sweet-making is the use of mutton fat instead of lard, which gives a better flavour. The name *polverones* comes from the word *polvo* meaning powder, because the biscuits are so brittle that they fall to pieces in the mouth.

480 g/1 lb flour	½ lemon, rind grated
120 g/4 oz lard or mutton fat , if available, finely chopped	1 teaspoon lemon juice
75 g/3 oz icing sugar	**Wine:** a fine heavy dessert wine from Andalusia
2 tablespoons ground cinnamon	

Sprinkle the flour evenly over an baking sheet and place the sheet in a preheated oven. Let the flour brown lightly, stirring several times. Remove it from the oven, allow to cool and sift it . Pour half the flour on to a work surface and make a well in the centre. Place the chopped fat , 50g/1¾ oz icing sugar, the cinnamon, the grated lemon peel and the lemon juice in the well. Knead everything together firmly and quickly. Shape the dough into a ball and place it in a bowl. Cover it with a damp cloth and refrigerate for 1 hour.

Preheat the oven to 160°C/325°F/Gas Mark 3. Sprinkle the other half of the browned flour onto the work surface, roll out the dough to a thickness of 1 cm/½ in and cut out round biscuit shapes, 5 cm/2 in. in diameter. Moisten a baking sheet with a little water, arrange the biscuits on it and bake in the oven until they are slightly coloured. Allow to cool and remove carefully from the baking sheet. Sprinkle thickly with the icing sugar and store them in airtight biscuit tins, separating each layer with sheets of greaseproof or wax paper.

TURRÓN

Spanish Nougat

Today these sweets can be bought all over Spain. In olden days, Turrón was a costly treat, and was made at home for special occasions such as Christmas or Easter. Each family had its own recipe.

250 g/8 oz caster sugar	2 egg yolks
240 g/8 oz ground almonds	1 egg white

Thoroughly mix the sugar and almonds in a bowl. Fold in the egg yolks, one after the other. Whisk the egg white into a stiff foam and fold it into the mixture. Lay a sheet of aluminium foil over a baking sheet and place the mixture on it. Press the mixture into a slab about 1.5 cm/½ in thick using a rolling pin and your fingers. Cover it with aluminium foil and place a wooden board weighted down with a couple of full tin cans on top. Leave the *turrón* to stand for three days, so that it dries out and hardens, then slice it into 2. 5-cm/1-in squares.

THE BALEARIC ISLANDS

THE BALEARIC ISLANDS

The Balearics consist of four islands, the largest of which is Mallorca, followed by Menorca, Ibiza and the tiny neighbouring island of Formentera. By now, most travellers and sun-worshipping Europeans will be familiar with the islands. Even those who have not yet visited them will have heard all about Las Islas baleares.

The popularity of the islands has had its unfortunate consequences, among them the fact that due to mass tourism the traditional cuisine has been largely forgotten, since it is unable to compete with modern "fast food" in terms of speed of preparation. Yet in the Balearic Islands, as elsewhere in Spain, there has been a resurgence of interest in rediscovering the old cooking methods, much to the delight of the traditionalists.

Despite their proximity to each other, the larger islands have developed their own individual gastronomic traditions. There are historical reasons behind this development. Menorca had 70 years of British rule, followed by seven years of French rule in the 18th century. Even before this, Mallorca was not without its share of foreign invaders. From the 8th century until 1229, the island was occupied by the Moors. It was liberated by King James I of Aragon, who is said to have thrown a victory banquet, albeit a meagre one of bread and garlic. Nevertheless, he is said to have declared "habem ben dinat" meaning "we have dined well". For the Mallorcans this was so significant that the phrase is remembered amongst their sayings and a castle built after the victory was even named "Bendinat" in its honour.

Mallorcan cuisine is rich and varied. The sopa seca, (literaly "dry soup") a kind of bean stew is typical of the island. Pork is the favourite meat, and is the main ingredient in two Mallorcan dishes, sobrasada, a spreadable, fatty paprika-flavoured sausage and lechón, sucking pig

Below: The water pumps used to be driven by wind power. Now diesel motors do the work.

Overleaf: Mallorca - Cal Truent on the coast.

Facing page: Mahón harbour in Menorca.

134

stuffed and roasted in am a manner similar to the Castilian style. The Mallorcan rice dishes , cooked with meat stock and saffron or with fish, game birds and poultry have an ancient lineage. Ensaimadas *are one of the few native dishes to have become popular with visitors to Mallorca. There are snail-shaped buns made with lard. Other sweetmeats include fancy cakes and sweet flans , candied aubergines and the local Mallorcan biscuits. Those who wish to taste these delicacies should wander through the alleyways of the capital Palma and look for them in the tiny patisseries.*

M*enorca is only a few miles away from its larger sister island and yet the equally good food is very different, and not only because of the harsh Menorcan climate. One of the specialities of this island is rice with mountain rabbit and lobster,* Arroz con conejo de monte y langosta. *Visitors to the island should not miss the opportunity of tasting a* caldereta de langosta *(lobster bisque). Wild boar proliferate in the island's extensive mountain regions. During the hunting season in autumn, banquets are held at which game and young wild boar are the main course.*

T*he loss of identity has been worst in Ibiza, the smallest of the three main islands. Prior to the tourist boom, Ibiza was one of the poorest parts of Europe. Dishes from this period include* burrida de ratjada *(a fish soup containing skate or ray) and* sofrit pagés *(vegetable stew). Unfortunately these dishes are generally unavailable in Ibizan restaurants.*

Pork and Pastries

Opinions about Mallorca are most definitely divided. On the one hand, the island can seem a nightmarish spectacle, with droves of foreign holidaymakers turning lobster-red under the sun, on the other hand, away from the tourist traps one can find idyllic beauty spots and tranquility, even in the summer season. A keen food-lover may even learn of "secret" cooking tips and traditional dishes that continue to be served.

Despite the flood of foreigners, the Mallorcans have managed to protect pockets of their traditional lifestyle. After all, the island, with its varied landscape, is capable of catering for a variety of tastes.

Wild boar is the main ingredient of many traditional recipes. This hairy, strong beast from the wild has a much better flavour than its pink, domesticated counterpart. In the *sobrasada*, a paprika sausage of spreading consistency, the strong, gamey flavour of the boar is encouraged. Visually the product is quite different from ordinary meat pastes, which look quite dull in cmparison. The paprika lends an eye-catching, although this is nothing compared to the taste. A proper *sobrasada* should be baked then spread with honey. This combination of sweet and sour is one which the Moors introduced to the Balearic Islands hundreds of years ago. Now we can take delight in this Mallorcan speciality whose taste captures some of the spirit of the island, in that it is sweet and sour, fiery yet subtle, two sides of a coin.

The *Ensaimada* is only indirectly associated with pig. It is a snail-shaped bun baked in pork fat. These buns are made commercially in several sizes from miniature to giant, and are also baked at home. A Mallorcan would suggest that the secret of their delicious flavour lies in the good quality of the air on this Mediterranean island. In any case, the dough is coiled by hand into a snail shape, baked and the baked bun is sprinkled with icing sugar. Sometimes it is also filled with whipped cream. The best bakers in Mallorca make their *ensaimadas* so light and airy that they melt in the mouth. As a result they have become one of the most cherished souvenirs of the island. It is a common sight to find tourists at Palma airport with round cardboard boxes in their arms. Many tourists seek to capture the taste and atmosphere of Mallorca by bringing home an *ensaimada* or two.

Without the wild boar, the Balearic kitchen would have been in dire straits. The wild boar and the semi-domesticated black pig is the truly the quintessence of Mallorcan cuisine. The succulent, well-hung meat was the delight of the British in the 18th century, who adopted and "refined" the dishes to suit their palate.

By all accounts, slaughtering feasts on the Balearics of days gone by must have been merry occasions. A special dish was made using the remains of the meat and rice and it was accompanied with plenty of red wine. At the end of these feasts, each guest would take home a hearty portion of sausage, liver, fat and fillets of pork. They can be said to have well and truly "pigged out"!

Left: Acorns are the
staple diet of the
"Cerdo Ibérico". They
give the meat an
unchanging flavour.

Below: From pork to
fat, almost every part
of the pig is used in
Balearic cuisine.

CALDERETA DE LANGOSTA

Menorcan-style Crayfish Stew

Serves 2
1 onion
300 g/10 oz green peppers, seeded
480 g/1 lb tomatoes
250 ml/8 fl oz oil
1 kg/2 lb crayfish
Salt
6 garlic cloves

1 bunch parsley
3 hard-boiled egg yolks
1 tablespoon flour
2 thick slices French bread

Wine: a very robust white wine such as Rueda from La Mancha

Chop the onions , peppers and tomatoes finely. Fry them in the oil in a casserole dish.

Chop each crayfish into 3 or 4 pieces. As soon as the vegetables are tender add the crayfish, salt and 500 ml/17 fl oz water. Bring to the boil.

Meanwhile, peel the garlic cloves and chop finely with the parsley. In a bowl, mash the egg yolks with a fork, add the flour and 1 tablespoon of the fish stock and mix well. Stir in the egg paste into the crayfish stew and continue to cook on a high heat for another 20 minutes. Remove from the heat, cover the pan and leave to stand for 6 minutes. Put a slice of bread in each of two deep soup bowls. Then pour the crayfish stew over it and serve.

TOMBET DE PEIX

Fish Soufflé with Vegetables

480 g/1 lb fish fillets (monkfish, hake or halibut)
Salt
1 lemon, juice squeezed
About 250 ml/8 fl oz oil
90 ml/3 fl oz white wine
4 medium-sized potatoes
2 large aubergines
3-4 tablespoons flour
2 large, red peppers
1 medium-sized onion

1 garlic clove
1 bay leaf
3 large tomatoes
1/2 teaspoon ground cinnamon
2 level tablespoons sugar

Wine: a dry white wine, such as a wine from the Valdeorras area

Preheat the oven to 180°C/350°F/Gas Mark 4. Cut the fish into small pieces and arrange them in a greased ovenproof dish. Season with salt. Combine the lemon juice, 2 tablespoons of the oil and the white wine. Pour this mixture over the fish. Place it in the preheated oven and cook until tender, about 30 minutes.

Meanwhile, peel the potatoes, slice them and fry for 10-15 minutes in some of the oil, in a covered pan, turning from time to time. Slice the aubergines, dip them in flour and fry them in more oil in another pan for about 10 minutes. Seed the peppers, keeping them whole. Fry them separately, in oil, then remove them from the pan and cut them into large chunks,. Season the peppers with salt and return them to the pan for a few minutes. The

vegetables should take about as long as the fish to cook. Remove from the oven and reserve it in a warm place while you make the sauce.

To make the sauce: peel and finely chop the garlic and fry it with the bay leaf in the remaining oil until golden brown. Then add the chopped tomatoes. Season with salt, cinnamon and sugar and continue to fry on a low heat for another 20 minutes. Gradually stir in the juice from the baked fish and cook for a few minutes more. Then strain the sauce, which should be of a fairly thick consistency.

Heat the oven to 190°C/375°F/Gas Mark 5. Layer the ingredients in a large, fairly deep ovenproof dish, starting with half the potatoes, followed by half the fish and then a third of the aubergines and peppers. Season each layer with a little salt and spoon some of the sauce over it. Repeat the layering until all the ingredients have been used, finishing with a thick layer of aubergine and pepper, topped with sauce. Bake for 20 minutes and serve hot.

LENTEJAS CON SOBRASADA

Lentils with Sobrasada Sausage

1 kg/2 lb lentils	250 g/8 oz sobrasada
Salt	
150 ml/5 fl oz olive oil	**Wine:** a full-bodied red
1 small onion	wine, if possible from Jumilla

Soak the lentils in water for 2 hours and then cook in plenty of water, until soft about 1 hour. Heat the oil in a sauté pan or saucepan. Peel the onion and dice it finely. Fry it until golden brown. Add the sausage and fry for a further 2 minutes. Add the drained lentils and cook for a few minutes longer, uncovered, adding a little water, if necessary. The consistency of the dish should moist, but not too soupy.

SOPA SECA MALLORQUINA

Mallorcan Cabbage Soup

There are two types of soup in Mallorca, *sopas liquidas*, the liquid variety and surprisingly *sopas secas*, a dry soup. The latter is only to be found in Mallorca. For hundreds of years it was the staple diet of the peasant folk of the Balearics. The following recipe illustrates the traditional method of preparation of this dish, using the unsalted bread typical of Mallorca. Of course one can use ordinary salted bread, without losing the charm of this ancient, much-loved dish, although it will have a slightly different flavour.

2 large onions	1 green cabbage
2 garlic cloves	1 loaf Mallorcan unsalted
1 medium-sized pepper	white bread, sliced
150 ml/5 fl oz oil	A few drops of olive oil
3 ripe, medium-sized	
tomatoes	**Wine:** White wine or Rosé,
1 bunch parsley	for instance, from Alella

Peel and finely chop the onions and garlic. Seed and finely dice the pepper. Heat the oil in a saucepan and fry the onions, garlic and pepper. Meanwhile, steep the tomatoes in boiling water, skin and dice them. Chop the parsley coarsely. When the onion is golden-brown, add the tomatoes and parsley and continue to cook. Quarter the cabbage and roughly chop it into small pieces, then add it to the pan. Cover with 1 litre/1¾ pints of water, bring to the boil and cook until the cabbage is tender, seasoning with salt. Layer a large shallow dish, with alternate slices of bread and the cabbage mixture. Pour enough cooking liquid over the mixture to ensure the bread is thoroughly soaked, then sprinkle with olive oil.

PAVO DE NAVIDAD

Christmas Turkey

1 oven-ready turkey,	200 g/7 oz ground hazelnuts
weighing about	600 g/1½ lb sugar
2.5 kg/5½ lb	Ground cinnamon
1 shin of veal	Freshly-ground black pepper
750 g/4 lb ground almonds	

Place the turkey and shin of veal in a large pot. Add water to cover and cook for at least 2 hours, to make a strong stock. Preheat the oven to 100°C/200°F/Gas Mark ½. Remove the turkey from the stock, cover it with aluminium foil and keep it warm in the oven. Remove the shin of veal from the pot,. Leave the stock to cool and skim the fat from it. Roast the ground almonds in a dry pan on a medium heat, then leave to cool. Stir in the almonds, ground hazelnuts, sugar, ½ teaspoon of ground cinnamon and some pepper into the stock and boil on a high heat until the liquid thickens, stirring occasionally. Strain the sauce and serve the turkey coated with the sauce.

FLAÓ

Cheese Flan

Serves 6 -8

For the filling:
4 eggs
250 g/8 oz sugar
450 g/1 lb curd cheese
A few mint leaves
1 tablespoon aniseed liqueur

For the dough:
20 g/ ¾ oz sugar
2 tablespoons warm milk
1 egg
200 g/7 oz flour
50g/1 ¾ oz lard, softened
1 fresh yeast or 1 packet dried yeast
1 pinch aniseed

To make the filling, beat the eggs and sugar until foaming. Break the curd cheese up with a fork and fold it in into the mixture. Chop the mint leaves and add them with the aniseed liqueur.

To make the dough for the pastry case, combine the sugar and milk and leave in a warm place until foaming. Pour the flour on to a board or work surface. Make a well in the centre and pour in the yeast mixture and the egg. Knead, gradually adding the lard until you have a malleable dough which does not stick to the fingers. Then knead in the aniseed. Preheat the oven to 190°C/375°F/Gas Mark 5. Grease a round flan tin. Roll out the dough to fit the tin, so that there is plenty of dough left over for the sides of the flan . Place the dough in the dish and press upwards a little around the edge to make the crust. Spread the filling over the dough, smoothing it down carefully. Bake the flan in the preheated oven and cook until golden brown on top, about 30 minutes.

ENSAIMADA

Snail Buns

The word *ensaimada* is derived from *saim* which loosely translated means animal fat. In Mallorca, pork dripping is used in the preparation of this dish.

40 g/1¾ fresh yeast or
1 packet dried yeast
2 tablespoons milk
200 ml/7 fl oz milk
5 eggs
1 kg/2 lb flour
Salt

200 g/7 oz pork dripping or lard, softened
100 g/3½ oz icing sugar

Wine: a fine dessert wine such as an oloroso sherry.

Allow the milk to reach room temperature in a mixing bowl, then add the yeast. Leave until the mixture begins to foam, about 10 minutes. Beat the eggs vigorously with a fork, then add to the yeast mixture with the flour and ½ teaspoon salt. Mix and knead the ingredients thoroughly by hand or using an electric mixer until it becomes a sticky dough. Cover the bowl with a damp cloth and leave it to rise in a warm place until it has doubled in bulk.

Roll out the risen dough into a long, fairly thin rectangle and spread the softened lard over it. Slice the dough into strips and coil it into snail shapes. Place these shapes a few centimetres apart on a baking sheet.

Preheat the oven to 200°C/400°F/Gas Mark 6. Leave the "snails" to stand for 15 minutes then bake them in the oven for about 25 minutes or until golden-brown. Remove them from the oven and sprinkle generously with the icing sugar. Allow to cool.

THE CANARY ISLES

It is astounding that the small land area of the Canary Isles should have such contrasting landscapes. There are the sand dunes of Lanzarote, which lie under blistering heat in the summer, a rain forest in the mountains of La Gomera, which are always veiled in clouds and mists, the green Calderas hills of La Palma and the magnificent, wild beaches of Gran Canaria. The altitudes range from the wide valleys of Tenerife with their rich pastures to the snowy peak of Teide, the highest in Spain.

This magical group of islands off the African coast. is blessed with eternal Spring. Few holidaymakers come to Lanzarote, Tenerife or La Gomera for the food experience, they are more interested in the climate. Nevertheless, the native Spanish-inspired dishes are not to be spurned. Those who have visited the Canaries know and those who have not may have been told or can imagine that the universal menu prevalent in all tourist resorts has been established here for quite some time. Regional cuisine has a hard time competing with steakhouses, fast food joints and pizzerias. Why should it be otherwise here when even in the meccas of cuisine, France and Italy, the menu is often not what it should be in the most popular holiday centres.

Fortunately, on all the islands there are almost impassable mountain regions which are not so easy to ruin, since they are well off the beaten track. Here, in modest, unassuming taverns, local dishes are prepared which keep the traditional Canary Isles cuisine alive.

One popular and simple authentic local dish consists of potatoes cooked in their jackets in seawater and served with mojo sauce and a fortified red wine flavoured with herbs .

Page 144/145 overleaf: The Anaga moutains in northern Tenerife.

Right: Delicious, aromatic bananas are one the great fruit delicacies of the Canary Isles.

There are two Canary Isles products which are particularly good yet seldom seen on foreign supermarket shelves. These are mineral water from Gran Canária and bananas from La Gomera (the latter have recently become more widely available). Canary Isles bananas are much smaller than their South American counterparts, but have a distinctive, memorable flavour, a characteristic they share with Canary Isles cuisine in which there is more substance than pretentiousness.

Gofio, Desserts, Wine and Fruit

Canary Isles cuisine appears Spanish only to the uninitiated. In actual fact, the culinary traditions are firmly rooted in the environmental contrasts of the islands themselves. The wide variety and abundance of fruits contribute significantly to the pot and pan. What grows where is determined by the climate and terrain and this has played a significant role in shaping local cuisine.

With the first bite, the connoisseur can taste the exotic in Canary Isles' food whose distinctive flavour stems partly from the fact that the island's civilisation has evolved far away from mainland Spain. The Greek historian Herodotus of Halicarnassos believed that the known world ended here and it is here that the Garden of Hesperides is supposed to have been sited. This is where Atlas took the sky upon his shoulders to stop it falling on to the world. It is only recently that these outside influences of the Ancients have been noticed. The cuisine of the Canaries was once substantially different from that of the Iberian peninsula. The situation changed in the 16th century, when the Spanish conquistadores arrived at this group of islands off the coast of Morocco. Yet the islanders have retained a large measure of autonomy and national identity. The original inhabitants of the Canaries, the Guanchos, were a simple people who sustained themselves mainly as vegetarians. Meat and even fish rarely appeared on the table.

The Guanchos cultivated barley and beans and knew of few other crops. They used these ingredients to make the local speciality , *Gofio*. The preparation is straightforward but laborious. The barley is roasted over an open fire and then ground. The barley flour is then mixed with fat, and water. Milk may also be added. This porridge was the staple diet of the people and was combined with other dishes. *Gofio* is basically a variation of North African couscous and is not so far removed from the Roman staple, polenta. Even today it is an important part of the staple diet of the older inhabitants of the islands, although the recipe was undoubtedly transformed by the arrival of the Spaniards.

Like the Moroccans - the North African coast is far closer than the Spanish mainland - the Canary Isles farmers would feed themselves in the breaks in their work from the gofio flour they carried with them in goatskin-lined bags. The porridge could be prepared and eaten wherever they happened to be at the time. The farmers' recipe for gofio is something like this: they would mix the flour in the bag with water or milk and then knead the mixture in the sack until it became a thick, compact dough. It could be eaten plain or baked as a filling bread, and was delicious when combined with tomatoes, sausage, bananas or herbs, so that it was either savoury or sweet. The natives also added Gofio to soups and often dunked it in red wine.

Gofio can be prepared in a variety of different ways, for example as *fritango*, a kind of omelette which can probably be traced back to Mexican origins. *Frangellos* are a very popular sweet made from cornmeal, milk and honey.

Another authentic hallmark of Canary cuisine is the hot sauce called *mojo. There* are many versions of this sauce. The salad dressing version is made with Cayenne pepper and garlic, but for those who prefer something milder, parsley can be used instead of Cayenne.

Most Canary island fish dishes are accompanied by *mojo* sauce. *Mojo colorado* caters for those who like spicy food. Hot red peppers are crushed and ground in a mortar with salt, garlic, caraway seeds, oil and vinegar. This dip is good with boiled fish as well as fried sardines.

Grouper, known as *viejas* is a common fish in the Canaries and its extremely delicate meat requires care and expertise in its preparation. *Sancocho* is a very well-known fish dish, served with potatoes. The *pulpo* (octopus) is cooked in a pot of water, then covered with olive oil and sprinkled with paprika. Sweets also play an important part in the cuisine of the Canaries. *El bienmesabe*, which tastes as promising as it sounds, is made of almonds, eggs, sugar and sponge fingers. Another well-known dish is *el ñame,* janus root with sugar-cane syrup and another favourite is the delicate *pan de cuajada*, a pastry filled with curd cheese.

Left: The vines in Lanzarote can only grow in protected basins of volcanic rock.

Below (1): Irrigation ditches water the land.

Below (2): The "Pico del Teide" is a volcano, the highest mountain in Spain.

SANCOCHO CANARIO

Baked Monkfish

400 g/14 oz coley or monkfish fillet	½ small chilli pepper
400 g/14 oz potatoes	1 tablespoon freshly-ground black pepper
Salt	4 tablespoons oil
2 cloves garlic	2 tablespoons white wine vinegar
½ tablespoon caraway seeds	

Peel the potatoes and cut them into medium-sized pieces. Boil them in salted water in a tightly-covered saucepan for several minutes. Cut the fish into pieces, add to the potatoes and cook until tender on a low heat. Meanwhile, peel the garlic cloves and pound them in a mortar with the salt, chilli pepper and caraway seeds. Add the pepper and oil and mix well. Finally stir in the vinegar.
As soon as the fish and potatoes are tender, drain off the water. Serve, accompanied by the sauce.

SOPA DE PESCADO

Fish Soup

2 medium-sized tomatoes	A few strands of saffron
2 medium-sized onions	2 potatoes
Salt	4 garlic cloves
Pinch of caraway seeds	60 g/2 oz ground almonds
2 sprigs marjoram	1 bunch parsley
2 sprigs thyme	250 g/8 oz day-old bread
1 kg/2 lb coley or monkfish fillets	Pinch freshly-ground black pepper

Steep the tomatoes in boiling water for a few minutes, then skin them and dice them . Peel the onions and slice them into thin rings. Bring 1.5 litres/2½ pints salted water to the boil, and add the caraway seeds and the marjoram and thyme tied together. Peel the potatoes, slice them thickly and add to the pot as soon as the water comes to the boil. Cut the fish into small pieces and pound the saffron strands in a mortar. Add the fish and saffron to the pot, when the potatoes have been cooking for 10 minutes. Reduce the heat and simmer gently.
Peel the garlic and chop it finely with the almonds and parsley. Combine in a small bowl until you have a thick paste. Cut the bread into four thick slices or into cubes and arrange in four soup bowls. As soon as the fish is tender, season the soup with salt and pepper and pour it over the bread. Serve with the parsley mixture and fresh bread.

GUISO DE CONEJO ESTILO CANARIO

Canary Isles Rabbit

1 oven-ready rabbit, weighing approx. 1 kg/2 lb	Salt and pepper
100 g/3½ oz breadcrumbs	200 g/7 oz sliced streaky bacon
500 ml/17 fl oz tepid milk	125 ml/4 fl oz white wine
100 g/3½ oz pork belly	480 g/1 lb onions
1 bunch parsley	3 cloves
100 g/3½ oz beef bone marrow	

Preheat the oven to 180°C/350°F/Gas Mark 5. Wash the rabbit and dry it thoroughly with kitchen paper. To make the stuffing, soak the breadcrumbs in the milk in a mixing bowl. Finely chop the pork belly, parsley and bone marrow and add to the mixing bowl. Season with salt and pepper and mix into a thick paste. Stuff the rabbit with the mixture. Sew up the opening with needle and strong thread.
Line the bottom of a roasting pan with the streaky bacon and lay the rabbit on top. Pour the wine over the rabbit and roast in the preheated oven for 1½ hours., turning the rabbit several times, whilst roasting.
Towards the end of the cooking time, peel the onions and slice them into thin rings. Cook them in a little salted water with the cloves until soft. Discard the cloves and mash the onions by pushing them through a sieve or grinding them in a blender. Season the thick onion purée with salt. Remove the rabbit from the oven and remove the thread. Arrange the rabbit on a large serving-dish. Pour the pan juices over it and spread it with the onion purée.

PUCHERO CANARIO

Canary Islands Stew

400 g/14 oz stewing steak	150 g/5 oz pumpkin
200 g/7 oz bacon	100 g/3½ oz haricot beans
100 g/3½ oz chorizo	200 g7 oz potatoes
100 g/3½ oz blood sausage	100 g/3½ oz sweet potatoes
200 g/7 oz chick-peas	1 tender cob of corn
Salt	1 clove
100 g/3½ oz pears	3 garlic cloves
100 g/3½ oz cabbage	

Soak the stewing steak, chorizo, blood sausage and chick peas in water for 12 hours. Drain, rinse, then drain again. Preheat the oven to a low heat. Put the meat and chick peas in a casserole pot, add 450 ml/15 fl oz of water and place in the oven for 30 minutes.

Meanwhile peel and cube the pears. Trim the cabbage and peel the pumpkin; shred the cabbage and chop the pumpkin into small pieces. Then add the haricot beans, pears, cabbage and pumpkin to the pot in the oven and cook for another 2 hours. Peel and dice the potatoes and add them with the corn cob to the stew. Cook for a further 25 minutes. Finally , add the crushed garlic, saffron and cloves. Ensure that the stew does not dry out at any time in the cooking process. If this looks likely, add more water.

PLÁTANOS AL RON

Bananas in Rum

100 g/3½ oz butter	2 lemons, juice squeezed
8 firm, ripe bananas	2 tablespoons chopped
3 tablespoons rum	almonds
6 tablespoons sugar	

Preheat the oven to 190°C/375°F/Gas Mark 5. Melt the butter in an ovenproof dish. Add the peeled bananas,. pour half the lemon juice over them and all of the rum; sprinkle with the sugar. Bake in the preheated oven for 12-15 minutes, sprinkling occasionally with the rest of the lemon juice. Serve hot, garnished with the chopped almonds.

CREMA AL RON

Rum Cream

500 ml/17 fl oz full cream milk	4 tablespoons sugar
1 cinnamon stick	3 tablespoons flour, sifted
4 egg yolks	2-3 tablespoons dark rum

Heat the milk very slowly in a pan with the cinnamon stick. Remove from heat just before the milk comes to the boil and leave to stand for 5 minutes, covered with a lid.

Whisk the egg yolks and sugar in a bowl until they are thick and foaming. Fold the flour into the mixture. Strain the hot milk through a sieve into the egg mixture, stir well, then pour the mixture into a saucepan. Place on a medium heat and cook, stirring continuously until creamy. Add the rum and continue to stir on a low heat for a few minutes longer. Remove the rum cream from the heat and leave to cool, still stirring to ensure that a skin does not form. Pour the cream into sundae glasses, ramekins or tall glasses and refrigerate until chilled. Serve with sponge fingers and fresh figs.

Spanish Wine - An Overview

The Spanish say "Comer sin vino, comer mezquino" - it is a poor meal without wine. This is hardly surprising in the light of the abundance of excellent Spanish vineyards. If you have any prejudices about Spanish wines, forget them. The present generation of œnologists and vintners produce fine red wines and fresh, young white ones. Some producers are experiment ing with new, international vine stocks while others rely on traditional Spanish varieties. Both approaches have the same aim, namely to produce wines of a broad palate, full of character and of international standard. The one factor which is still characteristically Spanish is the low price. A good Rioja, for example, is very competitively priced compared to an expensive claret or a Burgundy . Spain is a wine-growing country with astounding potential which invites adventurous wine-tasting trips. To be on the safe side, it is best to heed the advice of the professionals. Here is a brief survey which should suffice to tempt you to sample Spanish wines, if you have not already done so.

The Wine-growing Regions

Rioja, with its first -class red wine, Jerez in Andalusia, with its incomparable sherries, Navarre, with its Rosé which ranks as one of the world's best and Penedès with its fresh, young whites are the best -known and most prestigious wine-producing regions. Yet Spain has still more to offer,. It is worthwhile noting the names of the 34 recognised wine growing regions, the so-called *Denominaciones de Origen* (D. O.) regions. Some of the finest grapes of Spain grow in Ribera del Duero, Spain's equivalent of the chianti region of Italy, in the north-west of the Iberian Peninsula. This region exports the world famous wines of the Bodega Vega Sicilia. In the neighbouring vineyards of Rueda, Toro and El Bierzo, light ,refreshing white wines similar to German whites are grown side-by-side with rich ,red and rosé wines. The La Mancha region of Valencia, in central Spain boasts the largest single vineyard in the world, covering 480, 000 hectares. The neighbouring vineyards of Valdepeñas are full of promise; the grapes for making light white, red and rosé quality wines grow in abundance. The body and aroma of these wines surpass many a vin de pays and are very competitively priced.

Barricas

Spain ins one of the wine-producing countries which has retained the tradition of maturing wine in wooden casks and the best casks are made of oak. These imbue the wine with natural acids, bouquet and a characteristic woody taste. The Barricas, the equivalent of the French "barriques", are huge casks with a 225-litre capacity in which wine matures for 5-10 years in the major red-wine-making regions of Spain. During the maturing process, the red wines are switched between casks of varying ages. How exactly this is done is of course a trade secret of each Bodega and this forms the individal character of each wine.

Cava

Cava is the sparkling wine sensation of the Spanish hills. This quality Spanish wine is made according to the méthode champenoise. A top quality Cava is as good as any of the big names in Champagne and yet still has something quite unique. Soil, climate and vine stocks of the D. E. (*denominación Especifica*), the region in which the grapes are grown, give Cava its uniqueness. Today ,the name Cava represents a broad offering of fine, sparkling wines ranging from the refreshing "Brut natures", the elegant dry "Extra Bruts", ans the mild semi-dry "Semi-secos".
Cava is served in tulip glasses. The ideal temperature for "Bruts" or "Brut natures" is around 6°C, whereas the milder, semi-dry Cavas are best served even cooler at around 4°C. The dry Cavas are the ideal accompaniment to poultry, shellfish and fish. The sweet wines are fine dessert wines.

Consejo

Every wine-growing region is controlled by a regional Consejo Regulador, a committee responsible for the monitoring and maintenance of squality control standards. The work of the Consejos is standardised throughout Spain by the INDO, the National Insitute for Wine, which coordinates the work of the Consejos and advises them on all important issues.

Quality Control

If Spain, unlike almost any other European wine-producing country, have remained free of scandal, the reason behind it is this exemplary system of quality control. Spanish wine law defines quality criteria and supervision and inspection methods which are among the strictest in Europe. The laws not only establish to which analytical processes the various grades should be subjected, which techniques may be employed in the cellars and which vine stocks can be used to produce the wines, but also regulates marketing, the maximum yield per hectare and crop management . The opinions of the Spanish Consumers' Association plays a significant role; each bottle of Spanish wine bears a numbered seal, so that in the event of a complaint the wine can be traced back to its origin.

Standards of Quality

The Spanish wine laws also define the various grades, in which the origin, individual qualities, maturity and age of wines are classified as follows:-

Vino de Calidad - simple young quality wines which have not had time to mature in a cask or bottle. They must be made from grapes picked from vines within the permitted boundaries of the Denominaciones.

Vino de Crianza - under Spanish wine law, Crianza wines must be aged for at least six months in the cask and bottle. Only in this way do the special qualities of the particular D. O. begin to reveal themselves.

Vino de Reserva - high quality wines matured for at least one year in oak barrels and a further two years in the bottle. White and Rosé wines are seldom matured to this level.

Vino de Gran Reserva - Only the best red wines are aged long enough to be entitled to call themselves Gran Reserva and be labelled accordingly. They must age for at least two years in the cask and a further three years in the bottle. White and Rosé wines have to mature for a total of four years, at least six months of which must be in the cask. These wines are rarely encountered, as fresh, young whites and Rosés are generally preferred.

Vine Stocks

600 grape varieties are catalogued in Spain, but 85% of vineyards grow the most popular twenty varieties. The great variety of vines give Spanish wines their distinctive character and personality. Naturally the type of vine significantly influences the quality of the wine. In order to help identify the quality, the regional Consejos categorise the wines as "recommended", "ordinaire "or "experimental ". Recommended stocks are generally those which have a long tradition in the region and can be classified with a particular D. O.

Red Wines

Tempranillo (Cecibel, Tinto fino, Ull de Llebre)
The Tempranillo vine is the stock used to produce most of the famous Rioja red wines. Tempranillo wines have a deep, powerful colour, a well-balanced taste and a lively aroma. The alcohol content is around 12%. One of the safest points of recognition is the unmistakeable bouquet, well-suited for a long maturing time. The Tempranillo grape ripens at the end of September, which is early in the harvesting calendar.

Garnacha Tinta (Garnacho, Lladoner, Tinto Aragones, Grenache)
This vine is extremely hardy, and is grown in abundance on poor, dry , stony soil. The resulting wine has a pallid hue but plenty of body, with an alcohol content which can be as high as 16%. The strong, full-bodied wines are often blended with other types.

Graciano - Graciano wines are distinguished for their elegance, bouquet and aroma. They should be drunk young. As a rule Graciano-Moste is used in further blending processes, one seldom finds pure Graciano wines. This grape is found in the oldest vineyards and although no longer so common, it is one of the original Spanish vines.

Mazuelo(Cariñera) - this is a very robust variety with a strength of between 11. 5% and 13.5%, rich in tannin and tannic acid. The wine is used as an additive in small amounts to intensify the colour and prolong the aging process in other wines, which might otherwise be prone to oxydation.

White Wines

Viura (Macabeo, Alconon) - this fresh aromatic grape has become the origin of the most important of white wines. It has a high yield and is used in the production of fresh, fruity wines with balanced acidity and an alcohol content of around 11%.

Parellada - the Paralleda is a very robust vine which grows in the ideal conditions of the mountainous Peñedes. Parellada vines are fruity and aromatic, often with a low alcohol content compared to other Spanish wines.

Sherry

Sherry, one of the most famous of the world's wines is also one of Spain's most important exports. Sherries can be classified as follows:-

Fino - a light golden, dry white wine with a alcohol content of between 15% and 17%. **Manzanilla** is a special type of fino grape from Manzanilla, which only ripens near the coastal town of Sanlúcar de Barrameda. It is a light, dry wine with a hint of the salty-laden Atlantic winds.
Amontilllado - Amontillado comes from the Fino family, and is amber-coloured, aromatic, full-bodied and very popular. It has an alcohol content of around 17. 5%.
Oloroso - this sherry is dark golden in colour, strong in taste and with a mild, nutty aroma. It is generally available outside Spain as a semi-dry sherry with an alcohol content of between 18% and 20%.

Cream - This sweet variety of Oloroso is added to dessert wines in the aging process. It is dark, mild and sweet with an alcohol content of between 18% and 20%.

Sherry is a suitable drink for all occasions. The Cream sherries are served at room temparature and are among the finest dessert wines in the world, ideal after a meal. The drier Olorosos and Amontillados should be lightly chilled to 13°C and the very dry Finos and Manzanillas should be served even cooler at about 10°C; they are classic apéritif wines.

How to Drink Spanish Wine

For the red quality wines such as Vinos de Crianza, Reservas or Gran Reservas, select mature wines from Rioja, Navarra and Ribera del Duero should be served at room temparature so that the delicate suggestion of bouquet can gradually unfold. They are suitable accompaniments to meat, game and cheese. The lighter reds or rosés from Valdepeñas, La Mancha, Navarra, Valencia, Catalonia and Rioja, as well as the dry young whites from Penedès, Galicia, Rioja, La Mancha and Valdepeñas should be slightly chilled and served at 8°C to10°C. They are a perfect foil for seafood, poultry and salads.

Blended Wines

The blending of wines from various varieties of grape is permitted and is indeed common practice within a single vineyard. Wine made exclusively from one type of grape is actually very rare. Some wine-makers buy grape juice from various areas, and blend it to create their own brand. The proportions used vary from one wine cellar to another, especially in Rioja where all four grape varieties are used to blend red wine. However the grapes used in blends must come from within that particular D. O.; blends of wine from different D. O. s are not permitted.

Wine Statistics

An average of 35 million hectolitres of wine are produced in Spain, accounting for 10% of world wine production. Approximately 40% to 50% of this quantity consists of high-quality wines bearing the "Denominación de Origen", label, including sherry and fortified wines. The rest are marketed as table wines.

Recipe Index

Rape a la Gallega
Monkfish with Potatoes and Garlic Sauce 22

Reo con Almejas
Sea-trout with Clams 25

Riñones al Jerez
Veal Kidneys in Sherry Sauce 127

Salmón a Nosso Estilo
Galician Salmon 25

Sancocho Canario
Baked Monkfish 150

Sardinas en Cazeula
Sardines in a Clay Pot 40

Soldaditos de Pavia
Little Soldiers frm Pavia 130

Sopa Castellana
Castilian Soup 84

Sopa de Pescado
Fish Soup 150

Sopa de Rape
Monkfish Soup 72

Sopa Seca Mallorquina
Mallorcan Cabbage Stew 140

Sorbete de Naranja
Orange Sorbet 102

Suquet de Peix
Catalonian Fish Stew 72

Tarta de Vainilla
Vanilla Cake 116

Tocino de Cielo
Heavenly Soufflé 116

Tombet de Peix
Fish Soufflé with Vegetables 138

Torrijas
Poor Knights 116

Tortilla a la Murciana
Murcian Vegetable Omelette 98

Tortilla de Patatas
Potato Omelette 111

Tronco de Merluza
Hake with Clams 38

Truchas a la Navarra
Navarre Trout 62

Truchas escabechadaos
Marinated Trout 85

Tsangurro relleno
Stuffed Spider-crab 54

Turrón
Spanish Nougat 131

Vieras con Col
Scallops with White Cabbage 26

Yemas de Segovia
Segovian Sweetmeats 85

SOUPS, SALADS AND STEWS

Algeciran-style Fish Soup
Abajá de Algeciras 124

Andalusian Chilled Vegetable Soup
Gazpacho Andaluz 124

Asturian Bean Stew
Fabada Asturiana 37

Asturias Fish Stew
Caldereta Asturiana 38

Aubergine Gratin
Gratinado Berenjenas 111

Basque Tuna Fish Casserole
Marmitako 52

Broad Beans with Eggs
Habas a la Granadina 127

Canary Island Stew
Puchero Canario 152

Castilian Bean Stew
Judiones de la Granja 87

Castilian Soup
Sopa Castellana 84

Catalonian Fish Stew
Suquet de Peix 72

Catalonian Noodle Hotpot
Fideus a la Cassola 76

Catalonian Risotto
Arroz a la Cassola 76

Catatonian Spinach
Espinacas a la Catalana 76

Cod with Leek and Potatoes
La Purrusalda 49

Corn and Chick-pea Soup
Guisado de Trigo 100

Corn Pudding
Fariñes 40

Country Gazpacho
Gazpacho Pastoril 114

Fish Soufflé with Vegetables
Tombet de Peix 138

Fish Soup
Sopa de pescado 150

Galician Stockpot
Caldo Gallego 20

Garlich Soup with Grapes
Ajoblanco de Malaga 124

Lentil Salad
Ensalada de Lentejas 76

Lentils with Sobrasada Sauce
Lentejas con Sobrasada 140

Lobster and Watercress Salad
Ensalada de Lubrigante con Berros 20

Madrid Boiled Dinner
Cocido Madrileño 112

Mallorca Cabbage Soup
Sopa Seca Mallorzuina 140

Mixed Salad
Ensalada de Hortelano 99

Monkfish Soup
Sopa de Rape 72

Monkfish with Potatoes and Garlic Sauce
Rape a la Gallega 22

Shepherds' Lamb Stew
Caldereta de Cordero a la Pastora 84

Stuffed Peppers
Pimientos Rellenos 64

Vegetable Stew "a la Mancha"
Pisto Manchego 114

FISH AND SEAFOOD

Algerican-style Fish Soup
Abaja de Algericas 124

Asturias Fish Stew
Caldereta Asturiana 38

Baked Monkfish
Sancocho Canario 150

Basque Tuna fish Casserole
Marmitako 52

Burgos Freshwater Crabs
Canrejos de Río al Estilo de Burgos 89

Catalonian Fish Stew
Suquet de Peix 72

Clams in White Wine
Almejas a la Marinera 51

Cod with Leek and Potatoes
La Purrusalda 49

Dried Cod in Garlic Sauce
Bacalao al Pil Pil 49

Eel Basque Style
Angulas a la Vasca 52

Fish Soufflé with Vegetables
Tombet de Peix 138

Fish Soup
Sopa de pescado 150

Galician Salmon
Salmon a Nosso Estilo 25

Hake in Cider Sauce
Merluza a la Sidra 38

Hake in Green Sauce
Merluza en Salsa Verde 52

Hake with Clams
Tronco de Merluza 38

Little Soldiers from Pavia
Soldaditos de Pavia 130

Lobster and Watercress Salad
Ensalada de Lubrigante con Berros 20

Marinated Trout
Truchas escabechadaos 85

Menorcan-style Crayfish Stew
Caldereta de Langosta 138

Monkfish Soup
Sopa de Rape 72

Monkfish with Potatoes and Garlic Sauce
Rape a la Gallega 22

Muleteer's Cod
Bacalao al Ajonarriero 63

Mussels in White Wine Sauce
Mejillones al Vino blanco 22

Navarre Trouts
Truchas a la Navarra 62

Red Sea Bream Madrid-style
Besugo a la Madrileña 116

Rice or Noodles with Fish and Shellfish
La Fideua 98

Salted Sea Bream
Dorada a la Sal 99

Sardines in a Clay Pot
Sardinas en Cazeula 40

Scallop Pie
Empanada Gallega 25

Scallops with White Cabbage
Vieiras con Col 26

Sea-Trout with Clams
Reo con Almejas 25

Squid in Green Sauce
Rabas en Salsa Verde 40

Squid in their Own Ink
Chipirones en su Tinta 51

Stuffed Spider-Crab
Txangurro relleno 54

MEAT, POULTRY AND GAME

Baked Pigeons
Pichones Asados 84

Canary Isles Rabbit
*Guiso de Conijo Estilo
Canario* 150

Castilian Milk-fed Lamb
Lechaz Castellano 84

Chicken and Lamb Kebab
Pinchito Moruno 129

Chicken in Almond Sauce
Gallina en Pepitoria 113

Chicken Stew with Paprika
Pollo al Chilindrón 65

Chicken with Mixed
Vegetables
Pollo con Sanfaina 74

Christmas Turkey
Pavo de Navidad 140

Canary Isles Rabbit
*Guiso de Conijo Estilo
Canario* 150

Madrid-style Tripe
Callos a la Madrileña 112

Mallorcan Cabbage Stew
Sopa Seca Mallorquina 140

Murcian-style Stuffed Legs of
Lamb
*Cordero Lechal al Estilo de
Murcia* 100

Partridge with Stuffed
Cabbage
Perdiz con Coles 74

Pork Shoulder with Turnip
Tops
Lacón con Grelos 28

Quail-stuffed Peppers
Codorniz con Pimientos 65

Rabbit with Chestnuts
Conejo con Castañas 28

Rabbit with Pears
Conejo con Peras 74

Shepherds' Lamb Stew
*Caldereta de Cordero a la
Pastora* 84

Sliced Ham in Tomato Sauce
Magras con Tomate 65

Stewed Beef
Estofado de buey 41

Stewed Bull's Tail with
Potatoes
Guiso de Rabo de Toro 130

Sucking Pig
Cochinillo asado 85

Tripe with Chick-pea
Callos a la Andaluza 130

Veal Kidneys in Sherry Soup
Riñones al Jerez 127

EGG AND RICE DISHES

Baked Rice
Arroz con Costra 99

Basque Rice Pudding
Arroz con Leche 54

Catalonian Risotto
Arroz a la Cassola 76

Fish Risotto
Arroz a banda 99

Heavenly Soufflés
Tocino de Cielo 116

Murcian Vegetable Omelette
Tortilla a la Murciana 98

Poached Eggs with Asparagus
*Huevos con Espárragos
Trigueros* 87

Potato Omelette
Tortilla de Patatas 111

Rice or Noodles with Fish and
Shellfish
La Fideua 98

Rice with Turnips and Broad
Beans
Arrós amb fesols i naps 102

Segovian Sweetmeat
Yemas de Segovia 85

Valencian Paella
Paella Valenciana 97

DESSERTS AND SWEETS

Ampurdan Doughnuts
Buñuelos del Ampurdán 77

Bananas in Rum
Plátanos al Ron 150

Basque Rice Pudding
Arroz con Leche 54

Catalonian Burnt Cream
Crema Catalana 77

Cheese Flan
Flao 143

Cinnamon Crisps
Polvorones 131

Galician Pancakes
Filloas 28

Heavenly Soufflé
Tocino de Cielo 116

Orange Sorbet
Sorbete de Naranja 102

Poor Knights
Torrijas 116

Rum Cream
Crema al Ron 152

Segovian Sweetmeat
Yemas de Segovia 85

Snail Buns
Ensaimada 143

Spanish Nougat
Turrón 131

Vanilla Cake
Tarta de Vainilla 116

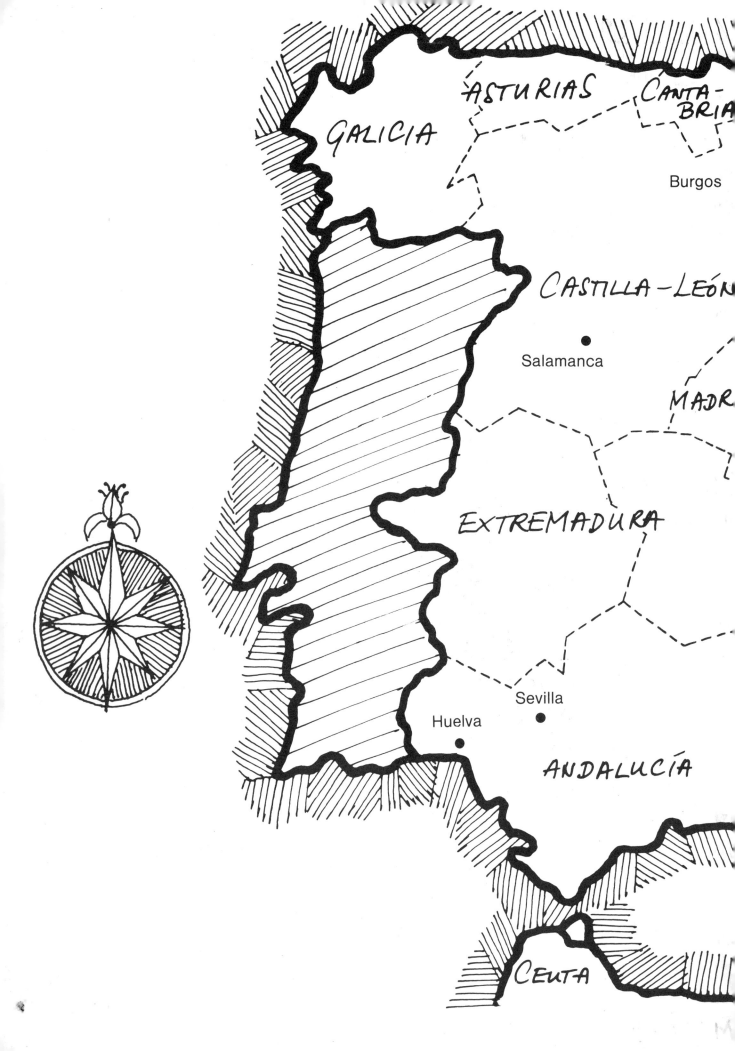